HAVE a NEW YOU

G N KARALAY

HAVE a NEW YOU

Mantra For Self Development

GOOD TIMES

GOOD TIMES BOOKS PVT. LTD.
New Delhi (India)
www.goodtimesbooks.com

Published by

GOOD TIMES BOOKS PVT. LTD.

H-13, Bali Nagar, New Delhi-110 015 (INDIA)

Phones: +91-11-25913301, 45069086 *Fax:* +91-11-45069086

Email : info@goodtimesbooks.com

Website : www.goodtimesbooks.com

First Published 2011

ISBN-13 : 978-93-806192-1-7

Cataloging in Publication Data--DK

Courtesy: D.K. Agencies (P) Ltd.

<docinfo@dkagencies.com>

Karalay, G. N., 1939-

Have a new you : mantra for self development /
G.N. Karalay.

p. cm.

Includes bibliographical references (p.).

ISBN 9789380619217

1. Self-culture. I. Title.

DDC 158.1 22

Printed in India at

Salasar Imaging Systems

CONTENTS

INTRODUCTION

My earlier book *Integrated Approach to Rural Development-Policies, Programmes and Strategies* was first published in 2005 in English by Concept Publishing Company, New Delhi. As the title indicates it concerns the development of the rural population (743 million as per 2001 census) in India which accounts for more than 72 percent of the country's population. The overwhelming response to the book made it possible to spread the message of the book to a larger readership when it was translated into two other languages and published.

Coming to the present book, in the context of the origin of a human being, whether one believes in Darwin's theory of evolution or not, it is certainly a fact that a man learns by experience. The greater his receptivity to new ideas, the more he improves. Also if a man makes a mistake once and is prepared to correct it, he will not make the same mistake again. During my service life I had occasion to work with hundreds of people spread over seven projects. I have witnessed many ups and downs in my life. I have also gone through turmoil on several occasions. Similarly there have been several successes and failures throughout my life.

In retrospect I feel, although I did well on many of the fronts which led to successes, I know I committed a number of mistakes too which led to failures. As a way to improve myself I took to writing down the thoughts which happened to contribute to my growth and also those which hindered it. After working like this for about 25 years, I thought I should share these thoughts with others. It is possible that many of them might also have had similar if not the same experiences. Even if there are variations in the situations or in the nature of the mistakes, on a larger canvas of human life, there are large commonalities in the basic nature of occurrences. Thus I thought that these experiences can surely help others in finding solutions to difficult situations and to help avoid any pitfalls that I had experienced.

In the *Great World Atlas* brought out by *The Reader's Digest* it is rightly said, "Man is only one of many forms of life on the thin crust of a planet earth revolving round the Sun-a minor star at the edge of the Milky Way. A multi-million starred galaxy, the Milky Way is itself one among a million other galaxies moving in the black infinity of space where traditional concepts of north and south are meaningless. It is a vision that dwarfs the globe on which we live and makes man seem very small. But it also gives him a new importance. For on this planet life has been created and developed, and as yet we do not know whether the delicate balance of conditions which has made evolution possible on this planet has ever been repeated on any other."

There exist innumerable species in this universe. The human being is one of these. The human being represents the universe in miniature form. The development of the human being is an evolutionary process. Many centuries ago, man used to live in caves and hunt for food. He ate raw flesh, tree leaves or fruits. Later he learnt to create fire and cook his food. He took to agriculture and learnt how to harness the available resources for his comfortable living. He started enriching his life by developing art and culture. This process has given birth to different civilizations at different places at different times. Various societies grew under these different civilizations. The progress made by these societies always varied from each other depending upon the progress of human beings constituting these societies. The development of a human being as a worthy member of society thus became the focus of research by many.

The personality of a human being is the most complex in relation to the animal world as the human being has not only consciousness but is also endowed with a power of discrimination, that is a power to distinguish between good and bad. In spite of certain comman qualities each person differs from the other in terms of physique, appearance, thinking or behaviour. Since the progress of a society is that of the sum total of the people constituting it, becomes imperative to focus on the development of an individual. Over a period of time there has been a good deal of research in the field of human development. However, whatever research has been made so far is like the tip of an iceberg. But with whatever knowledge is available, there is no doubt that tremendous progress can be achieved if we focus on the subject of Personality Development.

In the early years of life, the brain and other parts of the body undergo growth and therefore there is generally a direct relationship between age and maturity. Once adulthood is attained, the level of maturity is supposed to improve with age and experience. But this time around there is no certainty of direct relationship between the two. If two men have been living in the same environment, one may show tremendous progress in terms of becoming a good human being and the other may be a burden to society.

There are people who are ignorant about the way one should function as a worthy member of society and at the same time attain personal prosperity. Further there are many qualities which remain dormant in a man. These qualities can sprout when he becomes aware and starts nourishing them. It requires personal efforts to first identify these qualities and then willingness on his part to strengthen good ones and abandon bad ones. Some people often start grumbling about everything except them selves. Such people will remain static while others will move far ahead in life.

There is a definite difference between living and just existing. Existing means just counting the days of life and waiting for the fateful day. On the other hand, there are people who find meaning in their lives and they work for fulfilling that meaning. There are definite skills required to lead a good quality of life. One of them is to understand the cause and effect relationship and guide our life accordingly.

Apart from supporting himself and his family, a person is supposed to contribute in his own way to the welfare of society and strive to make the world a better place to live in. The world consists of successful as well as unsuccessful people. However if we study the life of successful people, we find one common characteristic and that is they have found the purpose of life and they are constantly working to achieve that purpose.

There is a good deal of literature which claims to guide people to develop personality. They advertise and market their material extensively. However if we analyze closely the outcome of their teaching, we find much of their material teaches quick-fix methods. They relate more to the development of style rather than personality. The effect of such teaching is cosmetic and does not help in real life situations.

The whole objective of the self improvement process is directed towards attaining success in life situations. Success however can mean different things to different people. Some may feel they have succeeded in life if their health is fine. Others may have this feeling when their physical needs or comforts are satisfied. For some getting well in the profession means success. For some, physical achievements may not be the aim, but for them progress in the spiritual field may be above all important.

While it is impossible for any human being to succeed in every department of life, it is widely accepted that a person who is devoted to self improvement will have learnt the basics which would enable him to approach any situation in life in a most constructive way.

This book is designed to offer creative wisdom for holistic personality development and for attaining all-round success in life. The book includes 13 chapters. Each chapter covers a distinct topic which concerns interrelated human aspects.

Hopefully those facing intricate problems in their life, may find in this book clues which may give them a lead to solutions to them and for those who are already leading good lives it may help them to lead better ones. In this book, an attempt has been made to put the darker as well as the brighter side of things in the right perspective so as to enable one to make right choices and thus manage life better. The book can be more helpful if the reader once convinced about the ideas mooted in the book starts working on them in practical life.

"Plant a seed and cultivate it, observing its inner nature throughout its lifetime. Journal what's within the bud, and gaze in awe at what's in that seed that will one day create a flower. Then extend the same awe to yourself and the seed that had you contained inside as well".

Wayne W. Dyer

ONE
Who You Are

Mental Characteristics of Human Beings

There are more than six billion people on the globe and each one of these has different mental characteristics. These characteristics become so much a part of our lives that we are not even aware of them. It requires self introspection of a high order to know this. It is essential to know these characteristics so as to enable us to improve upon our mental attitudes, our behavior and our actions. Although mental characteristics differ from person to person, each individual will reflect one or more of the positive or negative characteristics which are given below.

Characteristics

Paradigm on positive side	Paradigm on negative side
thinks positively	indulges in negative thinking
concentrates on the work	does work carelessly
possesses good memory	is forgetful
does work with perseverance	is easygoing
is sincere in work	is insincere
has strong willpower	has weak willpower
is courageous	is timid
is wise	is foolish
has balanced understanding	is biased
maintains balance in activities	is lopsided in activities
is knowledgeable	is ignorant
is decisive	is procrastinating
is effective	is ineffective
behavior is moral	behavior is immoral
has self restraint	is slave to senses
is appreciative of other's views	is fault finding, complaining type
is kind, courteous	is discourteous
is pleasant in nature	is crude
is unassuming	likes flattery
is candid (frank), tactful if necessary	is diplomatic, devious
includes others	excludes others
delegates powers to others	concentrates powers in himself
believes in interdependency	is either unjustifiably dependent or individualistic
shows maturity in thinking and action	displays immaturity
is sensitive to others' feelings	is insensitive to others' feelings
is forgiving	is revengeful
is silence loving	is noise loving
has concern for others	is selfish
keeps engaged in constructive activity	indulges in gossiping

is creative	maintains status quo or is destructive
has self-awareness	has no knowledge about self
talks straight	talks sarcastically
has vision	has no vision
is proactive	reacts, is firefighting type
is ready to change himself	is rigid about his ideas
is helpful to others	does not bother about others
gives advice when solicited	is judgemental, gives unsolicited advice
has good habits	has bad habits
is calm in disposition	is restless
is cool minded	is short-tempered
is democratic, flexible	is autocratic
is authentic in behavior	wears mask
has humility	is egoist
does not have any complex	possesses either inferiority or superiority complex
has patience	is impatient
has long term perspective	goes by short term gain
is optimistic	is pessimistic
is easy to get along with others	is difficult to get along with
is self-actualized	is motivated solely by material benefit
gives priority to important matters	fritters time and energy on trivial matters
assumes responsibility for himself	shifts his responsibility to others
is trustworthy	is unreliable
approach is logical	is illogical
is honest	is dishonest, is manipulative
way of life is systematic	is unregulated, messes up
lives in present	lives either in past or in future
views are pragmatic	is theoretical, impractical
actions are consistent	actions are unpredictable
is contented in all circumstances	is always discontented, is overambitious
spends money wisely	is either miserly or extravagant

As one runs through the list (the list itself is not exhaustive enough), one can relate to some of the characteristics mentioned. We have to bear in mind that no human being is either totally positive or totally negative. An individual can be in any position of the paradigm. These characteristics form a prism through which one sees the world.

It is not necessary that what have been designated as positive characteristics are always right in any situation. There may be some situations where negative characteristics with some modifications may be more appropriate, although such situations may be less or rare.

Matrix of Human Endowments

Human beings are endowed with four unique powers:

Physical
Mental
Emotional
Spiritual

No species except human beings are endowed with the fourth power i.e. spiritual power. .

The matrix of holistic development requires development of all Unique Powers. The linkage of the human body and these powers is given below.

	represents	expressed through
1. Physique	Physical Power	Body
2. Mind	Mental Power	Thoughts
3. Heart	Emotional Power	Feelings
4. Spirit	Spiritual Power	Realization of self

There is no either/or about the powers. Every power being unique in its own sphere, development of all powers is essential for the holistic development of man. The powers are so interlinked that the strength or weakness of one will affect the strength or weakness of the others.

Body, thoughts and feelings have to coexist for proper results. If body and feelings are there without coordinated thoughts, the result is negative. For example if one has a craving for eating sweets and the body eats them without heeding the good advice of thoughts that as a diabetic eating sweets will make him ill, it is bad.

What if all the three have a set of programmes of their own running simultaneously? If at one time thoughts are for jogging, the body is for eating sweets and thoughts are for a picnic, there could be real chaos. Could there be a cooperative solution, first jogging, then eating sweets and then going for a picnic? In such a situation, the best umpire is one's own real self.

In the above relationship, the positive aspect of one will strengthen the other just as positive thoughts and feelings will generate fresh energy, while negative thoughts and feelings will diminish the energy that one possesses.

If emphasis is on one particular aspect of life, we are likely to lose sight of many other aspects which may be equally important or at least which cannot be ignored. For example if a person spends most of his time on work, his health may suffer and his performance may diminish. For balanced development, one has to work for all round development

If we compare relative characteristics of man and woman or say father and mother, the father at times appears more thoughtful toward his child whereas the mother has deeper feelings about the child. This does not mean that the father does not have feelings for the child, it only suggests that his thoughtfulness outweighs his feelings. Similarly the mother's feelings outweigh her thoughtfulness. Thus/while the head dominates in the father, the heart dominates in the mother. The father's immediate reaction to his child's mistake will be to scold him. The mother will explain to the child with love how he should take care not to make mistakes.

Personality Type

As a broad picture, the question as to how should we measure the real progress of the country and its people has been engaging the attention of various world organizations. It was felt that either Gross National Product (GNP) or Gross Domestic Product (GDP) alone could no longer be considered a valid measure of progress as these reflect mainly economic aspects and are therefore not enough to reflect the status of the progress in a comprehensive way. In this context in the early 1990s, The United Nations Development Programme (UNDP) brought out the Human Development Index (HDI) as a valid measure of the country's progress. It encompasses three major components. Education due to its unique importance is one of these components, others being longevity (indicator of health) and per capita GDP.

Thus/HDI is calculated as an average of the sum of three indexes namely educational attainment, longevity and income. Individual Index is calculated from the equation:

$$\text{Indices} = \frac{\text{Actual Value-Minimum Value}}{\text{Maximum Value-Minimum Value}}$$

Minimum and maximum values are fixed for each indicator.

1. Longevity is represented by the indicator–life expectancy at birth. The minimum value for the indicator is 25 and the maximum 85.
2. Educational attainment is represented by a combination of the indicators of adult literacy rate with two third weight and gross enrolment ratio (i.e. combined primary, secondary and tertiary enrolment ratio) with one third weight. For each indicator, the minimum value is zero and the maximum 100.
3. Income is represented by real GDP per capita in purchasing power parity US dollars. The minimum value for the indicator is US$ 100 and maximum US$ 40,000.

It would not be proper to apply suo motu the above index to an individual as his personality development involves both mental and physical factors. Because of the complex nature of the task of finding mental development, obviously this factor does not form part of the Human Development Index. Some international organizations have tried to bring out a happiness index but this again is plagued with the same difficulty.

It is claimed that an enneagram is a scientifically based Personality Type Indicator and it is being used increasingly in recent times. In the enneagram a circle is drawn and nine equidistant points are marked on its circumference. Each point is given a number from one to nine, with nine at the top. These nine points are also connected with each other in a particular sequence by the inner lines.

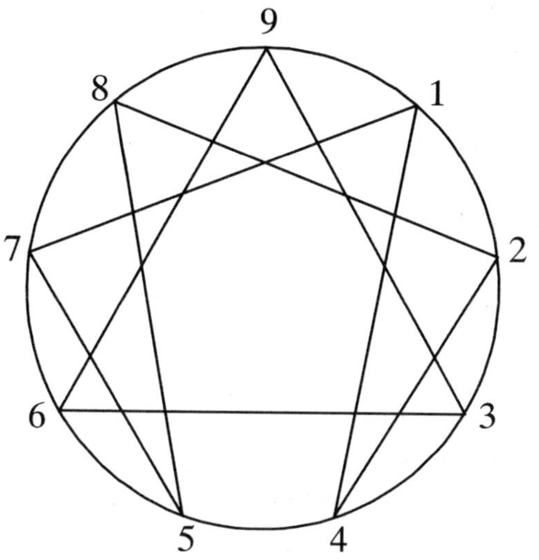

Enneagram

The personality type (with number on the circumference) with Riso-Hudson type names (indicated as in brackets below) and each name further expanded into four-word sets of traits are as follows:

Type One (The Reformer) is principled, purposeful, self-controlled, and perfectionistic.
Type Two (The Helper) is demonstrative, generous, people-pleasing, and possessive.
Type Three (The Achiever) is adaptive, excelling, driven, and image-conscious.
Type Four (The Individualist) is expressive, dramatic, self-absorbed, and temperamental.
Type Five (The Investigator) is perceptive, innovative, secretive, and isolated.
Type Six (The Loyalist) is engaging, responsible, anxious, and suspicious.

Type Seven (The Enthusiast) is spontaneous, versatile, distractible, and scattered.

Type Eight (The Challenger) is self-confident, decisive, willful, and confrontational.

Type Nine (The Peacemaker) is receptive, reassuring, agreeable, and complacent.

A few points have to be noted about the enneagram: 1) Some believe that people do not change from one basic personality to another. This appears to be a very general statement because we keep on hearing people saying that so and so has completely changed. 2) Each personality type may pick up traits of adjoining personality types i.e. say type Three may pick up traits of Two and/or type Four. 3) Not everything mentioned in the description will apply to a particular type because the traits further fluctuate constantly among the healthy, average and unhealthy levels.

Psychologists believe that the basic personality type is formed through genetic effect, pre-natal and childhood periods and influence of parents. Personality traits once formed unconsciously try to influence one's behavior throughout one's life.

The above description gives only an introduction to the subject i.e. enneagram and the subject itself is quite wide as it deals with complex phenomena as identifying personality type.

While agreeing with psychologists' findings, there is enough scope to change one's personality at any stage. History is replete with innumerable examples of people who have risen to great heights through personal effort. The purpose of this book is to help bring the desired changes in one's personality. A man is endowed with four powers i.e. physical, mental, emotional and spiritual. One has to be careful that not to lay overemphasis on any one of them.

"A good personality is one which enables you to deal effectively and appropriately with environment and reality, and to gain satisfaction from reaching goals which are important to you"

Maxwell Maltz

TWO
Adaptivity: A Way of Life

Objective of self improvement

Despite the general belief that human beings are among the strong species in mammals, we are physically among the weakest. Whether it is speed of movement on the ground or water, jumping in the air or sensitivity of senses, we come in the lower bracket of mammals. Then the question arises how did we survive so long? It is our intelligence that has put us in the reckoning. Intelligence has enabled human beings to adapt to the environment in which they are placed.

However, now the situation has changed radically. It is not as much a threat from other species which is bothering human beings, but how to survive within the human community itself. The challenges thrown by the advancement in Information & Technology and mass communication have put us on the fast track of life. We have two choices; either learn to move on the fast track or get off the track. It is now a question of adaptability to the new challenges.

We react to an event based on our perception of that event. It is not necessary that one person's perception may be the same as that of the other. Thus different people will hold different perceptions of the same event. For example, in a family the wife may differ from the husband about engaging a person to help in family chores, because both may carry different perceptions about that person.

Only a small part of our perception or attitude is inherited, whereas largely it is formed on the basis of our experience. Here again we form our opinion based on our perception of an event. If our perception is wrong, our opinion becomes wrong. This can happen if our opinion is not based on facts. Thus opinions can be different from facts. In the formation of our perception, our emotions play a vital role and these have the power to influence our perception.

How do we then bring our perception or attitude in alignment with facts and their correct interpretation? How do we relieve ourselves of the past baggage which is coming in the way of our progress? How do we identify our bad habits and change them? The answers to these questions and the remedies which are essential for achieving success in life are part of the process of self improvement.

The objective of self improvement is to enable us to achieve success in life and even more in fulfilling the purpose of life. While it is impossible for any human being to succeed in every department of life, it is widely accepted that a person who is devoted to self improvement will have learnt the basics so that he keeps himself on the right track while moving towards the destination he has chosen for himself.

There must be a readiness to adjust to new conditions. The world is undergoing a huge change. Evolution is taking place at a faster pace in every field whether it is social, cultural, political or economic. One cannot remain static in the face of new circumstances in a constantly changing world. We can't make progress in life with a closed mind. It is seen that children adapt themselves to any situation. The same kind of flexibility is required when one grows in age. Unfortunately some kind of rigidity creeps in as one grows older and the rigidity may be at peak in old age. However it is not that the formation of rigidity is unavoidable. With conscious efforts we can keep our mind open to accept new ideas and opinions irrespective of our age. We can learn this aspect better from a child's approach.

Change is occurring all over the world. Change is the essence of life. Everybody is subjected to change. There is constant change happening to us, both physically and mentally, from conception to childhood, childhood to adulthood and adulthood to old age. The quantity i.e. degree of change and the quality i.e. change for positive or negative may vary according to our thinking and actions. The pace and the type of change depend on us, i.e. to what extent we are averse or ready to accept new ideas. With fixed ideas, obviously no improvement is possible.

What is practical: changing ourselves or others/ environment

What we are today, is the product of thoughts harbored and actions undertaken by us so far. If we are not satisfied with our present condition we can always change it by changing our way of thinking and doing things in that direction.. After all this life belongs to us and we will have to take charge of it. Nobody other than us will think and do things for us.

If we have the willingness to accept change and we are ready to make the effort, we can certainly change. In fact such a change will bring enormous benefit in our life. By change not only will life be enriched but also the quality of life will improve. However when we talk about change, we mean change for the better not for the worse. Many a time even small changes in lifestyle work wonders.

Is there any particular time for change? Not at all. In fact no good thing should wait. Any time is auspicious. We must adopt change without any delay because it is easier to change at an early stage. Change is a continual phenomenon. Everything in this world is subject to change. Change happens at every moment. Nothing remains constant. Man undergoes a change: birth, childhood, adulthood, old age and finally death. It is better to effect change in ourselves so that we are prepared in advance to face the impending situation rather than waiting for the situation to overtake us, the approach that is called proactive.

Is it possible to change others? Generally we like to have our way in any situation. If we are able to convince another person about our view, it is fine. But if he is not prepared to get convinced, what then? When there is a conflict of opinion or interests between us and the other person, we feel sure of our being right and the other person wrong. We expect the other person to change his position. But the other person may be equally vehement about his being right. Judging unilaterally whether the other person is right or not does not serve any purpose. Having made our effort to convince him without success, it is prudent to accept him as he is and change our own course in a way that we feel is right.

It is not always possible to change the person with whom we have to deal. For example we may have to carry on with a coworker whether we like him or not. We may have to change the group if we do not want to work with the person in the group. On the other hand, to choose friends is our prerogative. If we are convinced that it's difficult to get along with a friend, we can as well terminate the friendship instead of carrying such a friendship as a sore.

Identifying areas of self improvement

If we feel our talents and potential are not being used we must look for change. It is not realistic to expect the world to change for us. Either we put in efforts to change the circummstances or we should aim to cope with them and accept them as they are.

If we do not like what we are doing, we should not drain our precious time and energy on such activities. Self introspection will help us identify the change required.

Our interactions with others help in getting a feedback about ourselves. Our natural tendency is to gloss over our shortcomings. We should instead try to improve our behaviour in the light of the feedback we receive.

It is unrealistic to imagine that the world or the people therein are going to change according to our wishes. The solution is to find what can be done by ourselves to change the circumstances and if they remain unchangeable in spite of our best efforts, we should change our own attitude so as to cope with them.

It is not possible to identify the change required in us without being aware of it. Observation is the tool of self-awareness. Let's observe the thoughts which are coming and going in our mind. This is like standing apart from our body to know our thoughts and behavior. We require deep self-introspection for this.

How habits are formed and how they can be changed

Genetic protagonists say that man's nature has been handed down from generation to generation and since habits are part of nature, they follow the same pattern.

A habit is that which we repeatedly do. It may be the way we think or the way we act. It is like a computer programme. It runs mechanically and is operated by our subconscious brain. Once a habit is formed it is quite difficult to change as we start perceiving security in following the habit. The proverb rightly puts it, "habits die hard." In day to day working, we develop certain patterns of thinking which make pathways in our brain. Our actions also follow the same pattern. If we are used to walking on a particular pathway, it requires an effort to find another. But once we do, we may feel that we should have found it earlier. It requires a conscious effort on our part to attain the freedom of choice and change the habit.

Habit by itself is not a bad word. If the species would not have been endowed with a characteristic of forming a habit, especially a good one, all of us would have to revisit the thoughts, issues and actions on a moment to moment basis. However, just as we clean our house of dirt and dust, we have to get rid of bad habits.

It is beneficial to us if we form good habits. The habit of doing physical exercise daily in the morning is good for our health. On the other hand, if a person develops the habit of drinking liquor, he is heading for a serious health problem. Now as addicts are aware, it is not easy to give up liquor. It would have been easier for him to leave it if he would have taken it for the first time and acknowledged no merit in it i.e. before the habit is formed.

By the same token, excellence becomes a habit for some people. A chef in a reputed restaurant always prepares excellent food as he has developed the habit of knowing the taste of the people and prepares food accordingly.

Our rational thinking suggests that certain actions are detrimental to our well-being. Even so we keep doing them time and again. Take for instance an overweight person who indulges in overeating. There could be several reasons for this: he cannot control his palate; his companion could be influencing him; he could be very happy or very unhappy; he could be under stress or anxiety or else he could be too weak in his resolve. Thus a habit is formed. However there are others who are able to shake off such habits.

Once a bad habit is formed we begin to feel comfortable with it in spite of being aware of its harmful effects. Whether it is sitting in a wrong posture or smoking, we are reluctant to change. We should make a sincere attempt to set things right as soon as possible.

We fail to take cognizance of a problem although it exists. Phillip C. McGraw in his book (P-131), *Life Strategies* refers to this as 'perceptual defense.' In some cases it acts as a self-protective mechanism. He states this as a mechanism that protects us from those things that our minds, at some level, determine we cannot handle or which we do not want to face. In certain unpleasant situations like trauma etc. this mechanism acts like amnesia (loss of memory) and is therefore helpful. But in most other aspects of life, this is counterproductive as we gloss over the problem and in course of time it gets worse.

Addicts habituated to smoking and drinking liquor usually defend the habits strongly, despite warnings, believing that they relieve them of stress. Finally they are afflicted with serious diseases.

The lesson is that instead of defending our perception all the time, we must check it with reference to reality and correct it.

Good habits are assets; bad ones are liabilities. Before a habit gets formed we should discriminate between them for our own good.

Habits are judged according to circumstances. For example, if a child has an outburst of temper, it is not taken in the same light as that of an adult. In the former case it will not be seen as unnatural behaviour but in the latter case, it will certainly create a bad impression.

As human beings, our thinking and actions are prone to be influenced by the company we keep. "Man is known by the company he keeps." It is often found that persons with particular habits become friends quickly. Habits like smoking or drinking alcohol transform strangers into friends.

Psychologists earlier believed that the behaviour pattern of the human being was formed at the childhood stage and in later life reflected the core behaviour formed earlier. On the other hand new theories claim that, though difficult, not only is it possible to change the old behaviour later in life but also that with experience man is better equipped to understand the desirability of a particular change and implement it consciously. This development gives new hope for parents who feel they could have done better with their children.

The proactive approach in adapting to any new situation can also be put as, "Change before one has to". This requires thinking ahead of the situation and calls for a willingness to change oneself. The chances of success are brighter with a proactive approach.

The first requisite for changing a bad habit is selfrealization. Next there has to be some motivation to change the bad habit. This will lead to a desire to change it and next to implement it. Success in implementation is directly proportional to determination and physical effort in changing the habit. Failure of even one step will keep us away from success in our efforts.

The repetition of an action forms a habit. Once formed it is quite difficult to change the habit, but it is not impossible.

A habit by itself is not bad. While a good habit is helpful for our growth and happiness, a bad habit is a negation of these qualities. There are some bad habits which lead to addiction. Drug use is a classic example of addiction. Determination and professional guidance are necessary to treat this.

Change can be passive or active. Unless we are determined to change our habit, we tend to follow the changed order passively. There is no permanent nor any significant benefit from passive change. Passive change is a half-hearted effort. Active change is that in which one is determined to leave the habit and implement one's resolution in all seriousness.

Change can be incremental and quantum. It depends upon the capacity of the person who wishes to incorporate the change or the matter which he wishes to change.

For example, if a person wishes to reduce obesity or weight, he has to opt for incremental change so that his health is maintained. Quantum change by way of too much reduction in diet or too much exercise may be detrimental to his health. On the other hand if a smoker or for that matter chain smoker wishes to quit smoking, quantum change in the form of leaving smoking altogether will be the most suitable option. Similarly for alcohol.

There can be a third option which can be termed as moderate change. This has more significance in an organizational context. Many a time, incremental change is found to be inadequate and quantum change is found to be impracticable. Organizations then opt for a moderate or middle-of-the road change which can be worked out in consultation with the employees or their representatives. It all depends upon which mode of change out of the three described above suits the circumstances. Timing and pace of change are important.

Willingness to change requires humility on the part of a person. Everybody has to remain a learner in one way or the other throughout one's life. Humility itself is a manifestation of a belief in one's real self. Humility demands courage on the part of a person to accept readiness to change if he is convinced about its necessity.

Bad habits can return taking us back to square one. What is required is determination of a high order on the part of a person to stick to his resolution. If an individual has made a resolve to, say, avoid fattening foods, he should make an earnest effort to keep it.

Accepting things that we cannot change

Niebuhr's advice and A.A.'s Serenity Prayer really go back to the time of ancient Stoic philosophers. The A.A. version is:

"God grant me serenity to accept the things I cannot change, courage to change the things I can, and wisdom to know the difference."

Albert Ellis, Emmett Velten
Optimal Aging: P-28

Note: A.A. is generally a short form of Alcoholics Anonymous

Whether circumstances are congenial or not, if we are accustomed to a certain way of life, we may not like to change. We start feeling comfort even in discomfort. We resist change as change requires effort on our part to cope with the new situation. In the short run it may be all right to get along with the existing circumstances, may be by bringing whatever (minimal) changes are possible to cope with the circumstances. However if the situation is not going to be promising in the long run, it is better to strive for changing the circumstances altogether.

There are some things which are not under our control and it is futile to persist in changing them.

We are governed by the laws of the land. There is no point in whining about these laws. However some people simply put aside these laws because they are unable to change their mindset, i.e. from being self-centred to becoming a law abiding citizen.

We have hardly any control over the outside environment. If something beyond us is changeable, by all means, change it if required. But if it is not possible to change it, effect change (for the better) in ourselves as this is very much under our control. The circumstances around us do play a significant part in the process but our own responses to the circumstances are more crucial for deciding the outcome.

Maxwell Maltz has developed a revolutionary concept called "Psycho- cybernetics". In his famous book, *Psycho-Cybernetics: A New Technique for Using Your Subconscious Power,* he states (P-37), "Cybernetics regards the human brain, nervous system, and muscular system, as a highly complex 'Servo-mechanism.' (An automatic goal- seeking machine which 'steers' its way to a target or goal by use of feed-back data and stored information, automatically correcting course when necessary). This concept does not mean that 'YOU' are a machine, but that your physical brain and body functions as a machine which 'YOU' operate."

The best example about the above theory is our driving a vehicle. While driving, most of the time we are engrossed in thinking about something which has no connection with driving, but we go on steering the vehicle subconsciously. What happens when some vehicle starts overtaking us with close proximity? Maxwell says the machine is operated by a human being and therefore he can always decide how it is to be operated. We thus adjust speed and the position of our vehicle to suit the overtaking action of the other driver. The principle applies to our journey in life too.

In this context, Maxwell concludes (P-246) by saying, "Make the decision to become all you are capable of being and to live a full, rich, satisfying life."

With great advancement in Information and Technology, there is phenomenal improvement in communication. This coupled with adoption of liberal policies regarding international trade, commerce and services has made the world shrink. Changes are taking place in social and cultural fields too. The pace of change is ever increasing. In order to ensure that we are not left behind there is no alternative but to keep pace with those changes. The way to achieve this is through changing ourselves because generally we have no control over others or the outside environment.

We must strive to change our undesirable habits and behaviour. With a proper approach, we can change these, and the earlier we do the better and easier it is.

"The mind is its own place, and in itself can make heaven of Hell, a Hell of Heaven."

Milton

Research indicates that the average person talks to himself about 50,000 times a day. And most of that self-talk is about yourself, and according to psychological researchers, it is 80% negative.

Jack Canfield

THREE
Positive Thinking

We become aware of thoughts when they take hold of us. But if we assume the role of an observer watching the entire process of thinking we can observe them as they arise, stay for a while and then recede. This is what we are supposed to witness during the initial phase of meditation. When our mind is restless, many thoughts will be crowding our mind. However, as we take note of them silently as an observer, gradually they will lose their intensity. In this process thoughts will still be there but we become detached from them. The longer this process continues, the longer our mind will be peaceful and will help us to become stressless. The process of observation can also be useful as a tool for knowing the quality of thoughts, whether they are positive, negative or just passing ones.

A glass half filled with water is generally taken to illustrate the way one thinks. Is the glass half-full or half-empty? Positive thinking will perceive it as half-full while negative thinking will look at it as half-empty.

It is preferable not to keep lamenting over unfavourable events. Focusing on the brighter side of life will give us positive energy. The world is full of duality: health and disease, beauty and ugliness, good and bad, up and down, bright and dark, positive and negative, and so on.

If we focus more and more on positive thinking it will become a habit. This can be taken as a reason why positive thinking is necessary.

Life means action and action is led by thinking. Thinking makes a man. Our environment together with our perception leads our thoughts to form our values. The values lead to formation of our beliefs. Our beliefs lead to formation of our attitude. Finally our actions are determined by our attitude. Positive thoughts will lead to positive values, positive values will lead to positive beliefs, positive beliefs will lead to a positive attitude and a positive attitude will finally lead to positive action.

Whenever our actions are at variance with our values, there will be conflict in our mind and this conflict will lead to an unhealthy situation. It should be our endeavor to ensure that our actions are in line with our value system and avoid conflicts as far as possible.

What then is negative thinking? Wrong perception leads to negative thinking and vice- versa. If for any reason we have created in our mind the image of a person as bad, we take it for granted that all his actions are going to be bad.

The assumptions that we carry have their roots in the experiences we have had in the past, especially the experiences we had during our childhood. Unpleasant experiences get entrenched deep in our memory and each time we come across a similar situation our thinking gets biased by these assumptions.

How then can we distinguish between positive and negative thought? The human mind is never empty. Thoughts vary according to our emotions and feelings. Thoughts can be classified into positive, negative and neutral. Neutral thoughts are merely passing thoughts. They are not associated with any emotion or feeling and as such they are momentary in nature. When the thought stays for a while and arouses our emotions or feelings, we can know whether the thought falls into a positive or negative category by applying a test.

The test is whether a thought or a belief is based on facts or truth and whether it is in our overall interest. If the thought passes both the tests it is positive and if it fails both the tests it is negative. If it does not pass the first test i.e. if the belief is not based upon facts, it automatically fails the second one i.e. whether the thought is in our overall interest. However, if it passes the first one and does not pass the second one, it is of no significance to us because it is not in our overall interest although it is based on facts.

Our belief to a small degree is based upon what we inherit and largely it is based upon our own perception of past events. Emotions and feelings attached with the event tend to affect our perception significantly. It is quite possible that the facts of the event may be different from our perception of the event. Since our perception of any event is fallible, our belief is also fallible. Our beliefs always tend to influence our judgment. Therefore it is very necessary to check whether our thought or belief is based upon facts or not before we take any action.

Dealing with past baggage

Though we wish to live today as it is, the past always haunts us. Our mind works like a computer. Our brain too, which works as an assistant to the mind, constantly processes and stores information. Both good and bad experiences get stored in the brain. Any thought or action brings to us past experiences. However, there is selectivity in this process in the sense that we tend to remember unpleasant experiences more often and distinctively than pleasant ones. This happens perhaps due to deeper grooves made by unpleasant experiences in the brain, which remain intact as a consequence of unresolved problems.

Unpleasant feelings are like garbage. Garbage has to be cleaned daily, otherwise it gets rotten. The effect of psychological rot is still worse because it affects the very thinking of a man. The best way would have been if we had resolved the problems as and when they arose instead of keeping them under wraps. However deliberately or otherwise, there could be times when one took a view, 'let sleeping dogs lie' or 'wait for an opportune time,' and we might have kept the problems under wraps.

Our present thoughts and actions are always influenced, in varying degrees, by the baggage of our past experiences. The best way to deal with the past is to draw lessons from past experiences and forget about the rest as in any case we can not change anything that has already happened.

There are certain decisions and events in the past about which we reflect now and feel that something has seriously gone wrong with them. The more we dwell on past events, the harder it becomes to stop thinking deeply about them. It becomes an endless cycle. In the process we miss utilizing the opportunities and enjoyment that lie waiting for us in the present.

Hamilton Beazley suggests ten steps to let go of regrets some of which are, changing thought patterns, making amends to thought patterns, identifying lessons and gifts from past events, and forgiving others as well as ourselves for what we think are wrong actions. It has to be understood that decisions taken in the past were based on our judgment which itself was based upon the facts available with us, our emotions and feelings on the issues at that time. We are only proving that we as human beings are fallible. We should, therefore, forgive and free ourselves of those regrets and focus on the present which is ever fascinating.

Fortunately or unfortunately our earliest experiences in life leave the deepest impressions in our memory. Our earliest experiences are childhood experiences. As childhood experiences are very important from the point of view that they impact our personality in future, we should take care of children from conception. An atmosphere should be created around the mother such that the child (when it is in the womb) grows in a healthy and positive atmosphere.

According to Sigmund Freud, the future behavior of a person is guided by his initial childhood experiences. Research shows that the brain is developed during the first two years of the child. If that be so, from conception right up to two years of age, is a crucial period. It is the duty of each parent to take full care of the child during this period on psychological as well as physical fronts.

Not everybody is lucky to have a normal birth. During early childhood the child undergoes varied experiences. Not everybody is lucky to be born with a silver spoon in his mouth. Many children face difficulties right from their birth, physically as well as emotionally. When this child becomes an adult, he carries all his childhood memories. According to Mark Twain, we are likely to remember unpleasant experiences more vividly than pleasant ones. Thus the adult behavior of the person, who goes through traumatic experience during birth and childhood, may be in disorder unless some remedial measures are taken. Modern research shows that the behaviour of a person can be changed with a conscious effort. Therefore instead of rewinding and playing the tape of unpleasant memory of the past events again and again, one should make a choice of positive thinking and right action in the present.

Childhood is a learning period and often parents are the teachers warning a child not to do one thing or the other. But parents also commend what a child does at times and express approval. However in general it has been observed that admonition of a child is oftener than praise. In some cases the child tends to withdraw and may even develop an inferiority complex. Another factor in such cases may even be the dysfunctional relationship between parents. The result can lead to negative thinking and even addiction problems.

Family and social factors influence thinking and often cause inhibitions. Finally such factors may lead to wrong decisions and a negative approach to matters. Understanding parents can make a big difference in their children's lives.

Living in the present

One clear message is : Don't miss the present by being in the past. We must realize that there is no remedy for the wrong that might have taken place in the past. Even the perception of right or wrong depends upon the situation and the timing. What is right in one situation may be found to be wrong in another. The only and the best use of past memory is learning a lesson from bad experiences so that the wrong is not repeated.

Thus without getting stuck by the unpleasant experiences of the past, we should respond to the present in the best possible manner.

Just as we should not be stuck by our past, we should not fantasize about the unknown future. It is not under our control. Who can guarantee that there will surely be a tomorrow for us? Imagination is part of our life and it is helpful but not fantasies. Most of the problems we face in life require a practical approach.

The future is yet to come and our actions today according to presumptions about the future may go wrong. We should always be prepared to take action according to the situation as it exists today and thinking fairly about their implications in future. But we should refrain from fantasizing about the future.

There is enough to think about and live in the present. Every moment of our life is precious as once it is past it will never appear again. We should therefore live it fully and enthusiastically.

There is nothing wrong in having reasonable ambitions in life. Ambitions help us arouse our potential which otherwise remains dormant. However, if we are overambitious, we would be stretching ourselves too far. Since we are ultimately responsible for our own life, we must break through high expectations and lead life as per guidance from our real self. The present offers us many things. We should learn to enjoy what we have today.

We must learn how a child enjoys his childhood and enjoy our life. If only we can replicate the characteristics that make childhood enjoyable we can enjoy the rest of our lifetime pretty well.

We are engaged in work for our livelihood as well as growth. Instead of treating work as a burden, if we do it with interest, work should become a matter of pleasure. Then, even failures soar above worries and vanish.

Some of the things may not be happening the way we wish. For example, a son may refuse to pursue university education and instead go for a vocation though his father strongly wishes he should pursue university education. Accept the reality and get along with your life well rather than dwelling on something which is not under your control.

Are we treating life as a burden somehow to be carried on or an opportunity to live with joy? We are not supposed to take our life seriously nor treat it as a burden. It is an opportunity to live with joy. In essence much depends upon what our attitude towards life is.

Accepting reality is also taking a positive view of life. If something is not to our liking but it is a fact of life, accept that reality and deal with it in a normal way rather than ignoring it. Elation after birth and mourning after death are natural responses. Let these run their natural course enabling us to shed unnecessary baggage.

Love is fondness or warm affection. The existence of a species is due to love. Just as cement binds bricks together, love binds all species together. First of all love has no boundaries. It is present in all forms and all species in the universe. Love can be between mother and child, father and child, brother and sister, grandmother and grandchild, grandfather and grandchild etc. Love can also be between a member of one species and a member of another i.e. human beings and pets or vice versa etc.

Love to the mind is like oxygen to the human body. One generally tends to shower love on the family. Instead of limiting the area of love to self and family, we should try, gradually though, to expand the area and include as many people or even other species as possible. Scenes of sages show alongside men and women, animals and birds sitting by the side of the sages and seeking their love and affection.

Irrational beliefs must be changed into rational beliefs to get positive results: Albert Ellis, a famous psychologist, propounded a Rational Emotive Behavior Therapy (REBT) as an application of cognitive therapy. He designed the ABC model:

$$A \times B = C$$

Wherein,

'A' represents Activating Events: adversities, experiences-past, present, and predicted aggravations
'B' represents Beliefs: attitudes, thoughts, assumptions, images
'C' represents Consequences: actions/inactions, emotions/feelings

Assuming one particular activating event (A) is faced by two persons (say X and Y), the consequences (C) will be different for one from the other depending upon what beliefs (B) in specific terms are held by the person about the activating event. As an example let us say the activating event is lack of money. In the case of X, the consequence will be depression if he holds the belief that more money is a must. Obviously depression is a consequence of holding irrational belief. On the other hand in the case of Y, the consequence will be taking recourse to constructive action to earn more money if he considers more money is a mere need- i.e. simply as a matter of preference and not a must condition. The rational belief is helping him to turn adversity into an opportunity.

Most of us often drive ourselves to convert simple needs into must wants and then stretch ourselves to fulfill them. Any failure in fulfilling the wants is followed by depression. In the process we lose sight of many of our important goals. Another error we commit is that we incorporate our emotions and misplaced feelings into the facts of the actual event and the consequence is that our perception of the event gets distorted. The remedy is to make our belief rational so as to get a proper perspective of any situation.

Our mind is like a pot. If the pot is filled with dirty water, the only way to get rid of it is to empty the pot. Similarly to get rid of negative thinking, we will have to empty our mind of dirty thoughts. Unlike the pot the mind by its nature cannot remain empty. The mind emptied of negative thoughts if not simultaneously filled by positive thoughts, will again be filled with negative thoughts.

Certain practices help us to empty our mind of negative thoughts and fill it up with positive thoughts. The practice of pranayam (a science of breathing) and meditation are potent methods to empty the mind of negative thoughts. Repeating words which give peace of mind is found to be quite helpful. Reading the scriptures is very effective in replacing negative thoughts by positive thoughts.

A prayer to God a few minutes before going to bed and after getting up from sleep is found to be extremely useful.

In all this, however, emphasis on taking a positive view does not mean we should not take cognizance of the negative aspect of any matter. Ignoring the negative aspect can land us in serious problems. If we pretty well know somebody is up to creating mischief, there is no point in getting associated with such a person. Knowing that fire is going to burn us, there is no point in going very close to it.

There is a difference between faith and blind faith. We can have unconditional faith in God because he is the Creator and Giver. However when it comes to relationship with a human being, we are supposed to use our discriminatory power to know with whom to associate and from whom we should keep away.

Once we identify negative thoughts that come in our mind, it should be our endeavor to get rid of them as soon as possible before they spread their roots and thoughts get transformed into a particular way of thinking.

While it is bad to harbor negative thinking, we should not concentrate too much on getting rid of negative thinking. We should always be in search of positive options to replace the negative ones.

We should try to separate the problem and deal with it directly instead of compounding it and making it bigger than what it is. The proverb, "to make a mountain of a mole hill" fits in here.

A person carrying stronger thoughts, good or bad, tends to influence the person carrying weaker thoughts when they are in the company of each other. Therefore one should be cautious about choosing friends. As a thumb rule, just as "birds of the same feather flock together" we should keep company with positive thinking people and those who are engaged in constructive work. Avoid spending time with negative thinking people.

There are billions of people in the world and many around us. Rather than getting engaged and then misunderstood, we should try to avoid people whose values greatly differ from us or whose nature is not compatible with ours. There is no point in expending our energy in getting engaged with people holding totally divergent views about everything under the sun. In the same way we should respect others' freedom of opinion about us and consequently their behavior towards us.

Self-image and self-worth are important components of a personality. The success or failure of a person largely depends upon what kind of self image he has. A person's self image may be falling into one of three categories. The first category is self image based on a sense of inferiority and insecurity. Such people either suppress their expression or if they express they try to cover up their sense of inferiority or insecurity by acting in an overly manner. The second category is self image based on an egotistic attitude. Such people usually are self centered, strongly believe that they are always right and they wish other people to fall in line with their thinking and actions. The first and second categories of people sooner or later head towards failure. The third category is those who have created their self image based on self worth. It is always good to carry a self image based on self worth which in turn is based on what has been achieved as well as what is set to be achieved. There is a world of difference between 'being an egotist or having vanity' and 'having a feeling of self worth'. While the former has a negative (based on inflated ego) connotation, the latter has a positive (based on actual achievement) connotation.

There is also a larger and philosophical angle connected with self image. Man is different from any other species on earth. Man is made in the image of God. He is therefore endowed originally with the same divine characteristics. He has however been simultaneously given the freedom of choice as regards thinking as well as action. He can thus choose either positive thinking and actions or negative ones.

Berating others is bad but berating one's real self is not less bad. The sense of self confidence and adequacy, which are so essential for success in life, emanate from the divine characteristics. On the other hand, the sense of insecurity and inferiority emanate from following just the opposite way of life. These opposite characteristics are the main causes for failures. One can, however, reclaim endowed powers by practicing positive thinking with righteous actions.

In working towards a balanced personality one must remember the role that positive thoughts can play in creating optimism in one's outlook. There is a difference however small between hope and optimism. Hope means expectation. Optimism means inclination to hopefulness and confidence. Optimism is thus a broader concept that includes hope.

It is natural for a human being to be optimistic. Amongst all, this quality has helped the human race to survive against great odds from time immemorial. It is next to impossible to achieve anything great without optimism. On the way to achieve the goal, there will be so many hurdles that ordinary persons will get discouraged to pursue beyond a point and after some attempts, may turn towards pessimism. Pessimism leads to depression. This should be avoided at all cost.

Optimism should however not be totally divorced from realism. Ideally there should be a healthy balance between the two. Optimism again should complement action and should not be passive, leading to complacency.

Hope, Courage, Sincerity, Humility and Contentment

Life is full of hope and despair. Hope keeps the flame of 'our wish for something good happening to us' burning. It keeps the flow of energy in our body intact. Despair on the other hand inhibits our normal thinking unless it is taken as a passing phase.

Hope keeps us alive, even in devastation. Hope is something that gives us inspiration and enthusiasm. It helps us to shift our attention from the past to the future. However, hope is not something abstract. It is born out of energy that we invest in.

Courage is one of the most essential qualities for a human being to be successful in life. All great men are known for their courage of conviction.

Sincerity should be evident in words as well as deeds. If there is no congruency between the two, it amounts to hypocrisy. There is a difference between sincerity and doing a job well. Sincerity is related to the mental approach and doing a job well is related to possessing the requisite skill to do the job. A combination of both these qualities works wonders.

We should be cautious before making commitments. But once we commit ourselves, we should follow them.

We sometimes make commitments just to avoid displeasing others, knowing well that the commitments are unrealistic, these just can't be fulfilled or fulfilling them will cause serious difficulties to ourselves. When such commitments remain unfulfilled, they become a source of enormous embarrassment to both the parties involved. Such situations can be avoided if we are careful while making the commitments. It is better to say "no" in the first place rather than say "yes" and then back out.

Humility presupposes our readiness to accept new ideas. It helps us to learn new things, knowledge, skills etc. On the other hand *mada* (pride) stunts our growth. There are instances in the scriptures that even rishis/*munis* (sages) have fallen from the grace of God because they carried a feeling of pride. In today's world a lot of emphasis is given to success. More emphasis is on gaining material prosperity and in most cases at the cost of mental peace. Success is a double edged weapon. Success can motivate a wise man to behave with more humility towards others. Success can also make a man lose his head: "Power corrupts and corrupts absolutely."

In life a little kindness and courtesy go a long way in developing a good interpersonal relationship. Its expression in family life is all the more relevant, as we tend to take any service from our family members for granted.

Life consists of smooth rides as well as bumps. However, because of their complexity, bumps outnumber smooth rides. Therefore if we take everything seriously we are bound to lose peace of mind and health. Loss of peace of mind and health affect harmony in the family as well as performance on the job. Thus it is a vicious circle.

Reading good literature and writing down thoughts improves our thinking power. Writing down a problem gives us a clue to its solution, which may not have occurred to us earlier. We are generally aware of our strong as well as weak points. Keeping these in view we can select some uplifting thoughts and write them in our diary. We can also write down the resolutions we have passed for our personal improvement. We can regularly read these whenever we find necessity for any guidance.

Seeing the lighter side of things makes life easier. Conflicts can also be resolved better with a little humour rather than anxiety.

A word of caution for maintaining a diary. Avoid writing down negative thoughts or highly personal references in the diary because generally nothing remains secret for all time.

Contentment seems to have almost become a mirage in the present competitive world. Contentment is a function of the positive state of mind. People who live in harmony with nature are contented. People are not contented with what they have or what they are doing. Some people believe that a feeling of discontent motivates a person to achieve something which will give them contentment. This is far from the truth. On the contrary discontent inhibits a person to act in a normal manner as it will make the person to either overact or underact.

Contentment is related to one's perception about need. The nature of need may differ from person to person. Whereas some people get contentment when their tangible needs are satisfied, others aspire for things that give them personal satisfaction of a higher nature. For example, in employment, good salary may give a person contentment. To another person, if his work does not get due recognition, he may opt for a job which may offer him less salary but provides him an environment in which his work gets due recognition. As mentioned, contentment is a function of the positive state of mind. It is not related to the economic or educational status of a person.

It is my firm belief that God or a super natural power has created this universe. We should pay our obeisance to the Creator and prayer is the best form of obeisance to Him. In doing so we will be cleansing our thoughts of a negative nature and our mind will be filled with pure thoughts. These thoughts will enable us to lead our life well. Thus prayer is a key to real success and happiness in life.

Dealing with certain negative attributes

Shadripu (six enemies): According to Hindu scriptures, there are six enemies of a man about which he has to be careful. These are *kama* (desire), *krodh* (anger), *lobha* (greed), moha (attraction), *mada* (pride) and *matsar* (envy). He has to win over these and find freedom from them so that his thoughts are pure and so also his actions. This can only be done through proper knowledge of these Shadripu, positive thinking and perseverance in practicing the right actions.

On the negative side there are certain factors that need to be taken into account. If there is anything which is perceived as danger, we immediately garner our defense system in the form of fight or flight response. For our primitive ancestors, it used to be a response to a danger from wild animals. But in today's life, it is in the form of day to day stresses and strains. Unfortunately these are found to be more dangerous than wild animals. Wild animals could be seen physically by naked eyes and fought with primitive tools. But stresses and strains are produced as manifestation of negative thoughts which are invisible and require insight which one has to develop to perceive them. In today's complex world, to combat stresses and strains is found to be much more difficult than fighting with wild animals. The result is that there is a steep increase in the number of people suffering from heart disease, diabetes and other serious ailments.

To take another example, fear is a corollary of negative thinking. It is a psychological condition often created out of threat perception of danger, which is usually unreal. It has a power not only to disturb normal thought processes but also to do harm in terms of physiological degeneration. Even its lesser manifestations such as anxiety and worry, persisting for a long time, have the potential to create serious ailments.

Of all the fears, generally fear of death is the strongest. Some believe that once death occurs, it is the end of an era of a man, never to return on the planet. Others believe, including the Hindu religion, in reincarnation. This cycle of birth and death is continuous till man by his good actions merges into the divine spirit. Research on the subject of death suggests that the discomfort that a man experiences at the time of death is more insignificant compared to the injury caused by fear of death. The right way of thinking is to treat death as one of the inevitable phases of life like birth, childhood, adolescence, adulthood and old age.

While we are on the subject of negative attributes which are roadblocks to positive thinking and the good life, it is useful to consider the role that anger, possessiveness, over ambition, greed, hatred and such attributes play in our lives.

Anger distorts judgement. Controlling it and reining it in helps one's ability to judge. Anger and hatred are self-destructive, possessiveness and greed lead to unhappiness. Anger and hatred against bad things is good; likewise a modicum of ambition and endeavor to succeed is desirable. Ambition to succeed in life is desirable but over ambitious people often tend to be inconsiderate towards others.

To continue with negative attributes, some people tend to keep complaining about others. Such whiners must look inwards at themselves to see where they can improve. There are some people who present themselves as victims in order to elicit sympathy from others. This does not always work.

Having considered negative attributes let us now see how we can progress towards positive thinking.

Certain processes related to positive thinking

"......the dream is not meaningless, not absurd, does not presuppose that one part of our store of ideas is dormant while another part begins to awake. It is a perfectly valid psychic phenomenon, actually a wish-fulfillment; it may be enrolled in the continuity of the intelligible psychic activities of the waking state."

Sigmund Freud *The Interpretation of Dreams: P-33*

Dreams can be used to develop personality: During the dream state, the conscious state of the mind is switched off and the unconscious state has free play. It unravels the memories of the past. Sigmund Freud has done pioneering work in interpretation of dreams. His work suggests that interpretation of dreams requires special knowledge. Though to a layman, most part of the dream appears ambiguous, if carefully followed, it does leave a message. One can use this insight as one of the important inputs to develop personality.

Life span is not so important as quality of life: When we wish anybody well we generally say "Long live my dear......" What is the idea of seeking long life from the Almighty if we do not make the present one happy? If the lifespan is in our hands, many prudent people may like to live only so long as they are able to lead a normal happy life, and not beyond. What is important is to lead a fuller life every minute. And if we take care of minutes, the years will take care of themselves. Therefore if we have to offer somebody our best wishes, it is better to wish him joyful, happy or quality life rather than long life.

Taking charge of one's life is important. So long as we take care of ourselves, it becomes easier to take care of others.

But instead of taking care of ourselves, if we start meeting demands and desires of others, we may suffer and we may suffer to the extent that we may require others' help.

This does not mean that we should not take care of our old parents or dear ones requiring healthcare etc. who are helpless. What is meant here is that it would be much easier for us to serve them better if we take care of our own lives.

Our physiology has an intimate connection with our thoughts. If we are filled with positive thoughts, we feel strong and energetic, our appetite increases, we feel happy, we become interested in interacting with others. When we indulge in negative thoughts for long, we feel depressed, our digestion suffers, our stomach aches, our heart rate increases, we get headaches, we become sleepless.

Negative thoughts depress the mind and drain out energy. No positive and effective actions are expected to follow such thoughts. In effect our thoughts create our experiences.

In conclusion, it is good to know what positive thinking is. We should be able to sift the facts and use our discrimination to conclude whether something is good for us or not. This knowledge lays the foundation for our actions which are to follow. However if we take this knowledge as an intellectual pursuit alone, we will not be able to achieve anything worthwhile. There is no dearth of pundits who possess excellent knowledge but do not practice even the basic tenets of life. In this case even a person who has no knowledge but follows the right path is a much better human being.

The practical application of positive thinking is thus essential. Only regular practice of the principles underlying positive thinking will enable us to achieve real success in life. The proverb, "Practice makes man perfect" is more relevant here.

It is well said that thinking makes a man because we always tend to be led by our thoughts. Thoughts are so powerful that they affect our physiology also. The cause of many of the ills is found to be stress generated as a result of negative thinking. When we identify any negative thought, it should be replaced by a positive thought because the mind cannot remain empty even for a moment. In this context, affirmations (refer Appendix) play an important role in reinforcing positive thinking.

There is no point in living in the past. We should learn lessons from it and move ahead. There is also no point in fantasizing about the future because it not under our control. We should believe only in the present and enjoy its every moment.

We form our beliefs based on our perception. The beliefs may or may not be based on facts. The conflict occurs when two persons differ in their perception of the very same event. It is wrong to assume that our perception of the event alone is right. Life on earth is full of complexities and we will always be facing one or the other tough problem. However with positive thinking we are better prepared to face these problems. Positive thinking will also make our journey through life much more enjoyable.

"Growth is not only about getting healthy but about learning ways of living as well."

Henry Cloud

FOUR
You and Your Body

Physical wellbeing is the foundation on which the superstructure of one's personality and success in life is rested. It is therefore as important an aspect as mental soundness. It is a matter of common knowledge that even a headache affects our functioning, leave alone disease.

While maintenance and improvement of health covers a wide range of aspects, broadly the following are more important:

- Developing positive mental attitude
- Managing stress
- Managing obesity/ weight

- Maintaining *bramhacharya* or celibacy
- Maintaining health as one grows in age
- Exposure to sunshine and breathing fresh air
- Eating proper diet
- Doing regular exercise/Yoga
- Taking proper rest and enjoying recreation
- Maintaining hygiene

The aspect of developing a positive mental attitude has been extensively dealt with in Chapter 3: Positive Thinking. The other aspects, namely, managing stress, managing obesity/weight, maintaining bramhacharya or celibacy and maintaining health as one grows in age are dealt with here for the simple reason that, in the context of the present life style, these have acquired special significance. The other aspects mentioned above though important have not been dealt with here due to space constraint.

Being Healthy

Knowing the basics of our body and health are prerequisites for personality development.

There is a need to go beyond medical science to know about the body. In this context, the following is incorporated from the Hindu scriptures:

"The gross or physical body consists of five elements namely: earth, water, fire, air and aakash (ether). The physical body operates through five senses of knowledge - sight, taste, smell, hearing and touch and five sense organs - organs of speech (mouth), locomotion (feet), grasping (hands), excretion (anus), and procreation (genital organs). There is an astral body. The astral cerebrospinal axis contains six subtle centers or chakras. The power from the soul comes to the astral body. It is the mind which, on the basis of that power, gives orders to the physical body through five senses of knowledge and five sense organs. The breath is the connecting link between the soul/astral body and the gross body. As the breath stops, the gross body becomes dead and the soul/astral body wafts away."

The five elements mentioned above are of vital importance to our body. The salient features of these elements are given below:

Aakash (Ether) element: The *Aakash* element is situated in the inner cellular spaces of our body. While *Pranayam* and deep breathing replenish this element in our body, overeating diminishes its strength.

Air element: Oxygen is required to purify our blood. We get oxygen through the air that we inhale. It is therefore necessary that the air we breathe should be rich in oxygen.

Fire element: The fire element is necessary for the process of digestion of food that we eat as well as to keep the body warm so that our metabolism functions properly. The greatest source of the fire element is the sun through its rays.

Water element: Water accounts for more than two-thirds of the volume of our body. It is necessary to keep the balance of this element for maintaining proper functioning of our metabolism as well as temperature. The body becomes fresh and agile with the use of good water.

Earth element: The body has an intimate connection with this element and is very important for our well being. The sources of the earth element are food that we eat as well as earth/mud with different applications. The use of mudpacks on our body parts and walking barefoot on wet earth replenish this element in a big way.

The importance of the five elements can be gauged from plant life as well. The plant which receives sunshine, water, earth, breeze etc. grows better than if it is under the shadow of a tree. These elements can also be harnessed to get the energy required for our life and in such a situation the dependence on food can be reduced. There are examples which narrate certain human beings were living without food for long periods. Besides possessing indomitable will power, they mastered the art of separating N2 from the air, enabling the process of producing protein.

In order to keep the physical body healthy, it is necessary to keep proper balance of these elements and sense organs.

Health

The physical aspect in a broader sense relates to one's physique and simply as health. Even in Maslow's hierarchy of needs, represented as a pyramid, physiological needs form the base, which indicates their importance. The progress of a person largely depends upon the quality of his health although the world is replete with examples defying this general rule. One of the living examples is Stephen Hawking whose vital body parts are paralysed but he is still contributing to scientific investigation. But such examples can be termed as exceptions to the rule.

There is no scripture wherein it is mentioned that any other aspect of life has precedence over health. In Hindu scriptures, "The Body *Yajna*" i.e. "to keep the body healthy" is one of the five types of religious duties (sacrifices- *Yajnas*). Health is the most precious gift given to us by God. We should preserve it by all means at our command.

Good health acts as a sound foundation on which life's duties and pursuits are built. Good health also becomes necessary so that we do not become a burden to others. Preventive measures or timely interventions make the task of maintaining good health easier.

The World Health Organisation (WHO) in 1948 has defined health as follows: "Health is a state of complete physical, mental and social well-being and not merely an absence of disease or infirmity." The definition has since been enlarged to include, "ability to lead a socially and economically productive life."

Health (longevity as an indicator of health) is also one of the three components of the Human Development Index (HDI) brought out by the United Nations Development Programme (UNDP) in the early 1990s.

Managing Stress: A new approach

If there is any single cause for maximum ailments in the world, it is stress. Name any disease and it is found that either it is caused by stress or the condition of the person afflicted by the disease is aggravated by stress. Industrial and economic revolutions have benefited people in terms of creating comfort but at the same time they have brought new problems to humanity. The heart problem, which is the foremost killer disease presently, is directly related to stress. Coping with stressors has now become the major preoccupation of a human being.

Stress is physical and mental tension. It is a body and mental reaction to the stimulus causing stress called stressor. Stressor is an object or event which causes stress. The stressor can be external to the body; it can also be internal. In the context of stress, we can compare our body to a coiled spring. When we stretch the spring, it is under tension and creates strain. If we release the spring, it is restored to its original position. However, if the spring is kept in a stretched position for a long time, the spring undergoes deformation, the extent of which depends upon the duration of the stretch.

If the body remains under stress for a length of time, it becomes susceptible to disease depending upon the duration of the stress. If the stressor creates conditions beyond the capacity of the body to bear, the person can have even fatal consequences.

There is a variety of external stressors. These could be: quarreling neighbours, nagging spouses, demanding bosses, loud noise and pollution. We have little control over external factors. The internal stressors are negative thinking which includes anger, greed, anxiety, worry, fear, hatred, guilt or victim consciousness, limitless desires and attachments etc. Internal stressors are as bad as external ones.

There has been a lot of research on the subject of the effect of stress on our body. The research indicates that most diseases are either directly related to stress or they find their trigger in stress.

Sometimes, stress damages the body more than accidents. Stress works silently on the body organs and symptoms of the effect are not apparent to the person till his condition gets worse. Stress has to be taken care of well in time.

Stress is an outcome of our improper reaction to situations. We should learn to undertake all activities in a most natural way rather than straining our nerves. Physical overwork is not as much detrimental to health as mental worry. Of all the causes for producing stress, constant mental worry is the main one. Worrying becomes our habit when we constantly indulge in pessimistic and defeatist thoughts.

The best way of dealing with worry is to take a break every now and then from our duties and responsibilities. We should contemplate every day for about ten minutes prior to going to bed at night. When we pray to God, our subconscious mind will be filled with thoughts of hope and happiness which will find reflection in sound sleep. We may practice the same thing after waking up, may be for a few minutes. This will be a great start for the day.

Fatigue and monotony at times become causes of stress. Repeating words or verses from one's scriptures often helps attain peace of mind. Silence observed for a period of time is another such method to calm one's mind.

Pent up feelings cause stress. Relief can come if one shares such feelings with others. Anger, like stress causes tension.

Psychologically forgiveness helps to dissipate anger and its attendant bad effects. However forgiveness is different from forgetting the wrong doing. There is no need to forget the wrong doing when we forgive the person who does wrong to us. If we forget, he may commit the wrong again.

There is an old maxim: "Never put off till tomorrow what you can do today". We are called upon to do multifarious jobs day in and day out. The pressure of work culminating in hectic activities creates undesirable stress and fatigue in our body and mind. Since the time at our disposal has a certain limit, the only way to do it is to plan our work. Planning work in advance and organizing the work help not only to succeed but also to avoid strain. Both fatigue and stress can be avoided by properly planning our work.

It should be our attempt to finish the day's work on that day instead of postponing it for the next day. If we postpone, work will get accumulated and it will strain our nerves.

Stress is also caused by trying to do too many things at a time. If we do, we may not be doing justice to any one in particular. There are, of course, occasions on which we have to do simultaneously two or three items of work. Both conditions i.e. overwork and underwork are undesirable for health in the long run.

Emotions can keep us healthy or make us sick depending upon whether they are positive or negative. Our real nature is in perfect balance but emotions which are generated as a result of anxiety, worry, fear, resentment and obsessions disturb that balance draining our vitality.

One can conserve energy by maintaining a well balanced emotional life. On the other hand, disturbing emotions create such chemical changes in the body that can lead to physical deterioration. Anger is the major culprit in this respect unless it is an expression of the right kind and expressed at the appropriate time with an intention to correct the wrong. Generally, letting go of anger and finding constructive ways to face the difficulties of life is as important to our health as nutrition and physical exercise.

The monotony of life creates staleness which diminishes energy. Such a situation can be improved by incorporating changes in routine and relaxing by taking small breaks. Being in the open air even for a while refreshes the body and mind. Life has become extremely demanding in the present complex world. If we wish to live happily, it is most essential to know how to relax. But relaxation here means both physical and mental relaxation. . Normally most of us try to relax physically and mental relaxation is ignored. Without mental relaxation, it is not even halfway.

Being serious in dealing with important issues is understood. But we often tend to treat even less important issues seriously. This approach causes anxiety and stress. The fast pace of present life is increasing the stress to a dangerous level. While it may not be possible to avoid working hard, one needs to deliberately slow down the pace of activities on occasions when one is faced with too much pressure. This is necessary even for those whose lives are well organized.

Managing Obesity : A pragmatic approach

Why is it necessary to maintain weight? Mahatma Gandhi says (source: *The Encyclopaedia of Gandhian Thoughts* by Hingorani, P 24):

"It is more important for man to look after his soul than his body. A brave soul often inhabits a lean body. After a certain stage, the flesh diminishes in proportion to the growth of the soul. A perfectly healthy body may be very fleshless. A muscular body is often heir to many an ill."

Overweight is found to be a cause of aggravation of many diseases like those of the heart, diabetes etc. Obviously it puts stress on every body muscle and joint and as one gets older the mobility of a person gets diminished. More obesity generates more hunger. More intake of food requires more exercise but the body's capability to exercise diminishes as one becomes older. Thus it becomes a vicious circle.

There are mainly two methods to find the average weight one should have. One method relates to age, height and body frame. The Life Insurance Corporation of India follows this method. The other method is called Body Mass Index which has height and body frame as a criterion but not age. At the international level the Body Mass Index is followed.

Putting more energy into the body than can be used results in deposition of fat and consequently increase in weight. The diet has to be well balanced so that the requirements of the body in terms of calorie intake and nutrition are met. The daily calorie requirement of a person with average metabolism would be as follows:

Daily Calorie Requirement of Person with Average Metabolism

Person	Light work	Medium work	Heavy work
Men	2200	2800	3400
Women	1900	2200	2800

Source: Healthy Living by A. P. Dewan

Energy is measured in terms of calories. The calorie requirement of a sedentary person can be as low as 1200. The best way to arrive at the right calorie level is by monitoring the weight. Once a certain weight is benchmarked, the diet that maintains the weight at the same level over a period of time will give the measure of right calorie intake. In a period of time, the intake of 3000 calories over and above the body requirement will increase the body weight by 1 kg. and if the intake is less by 3500 calories than the body requirement, it will reduce the body weight by 1 kg.

Among all species the human being is the only one who indulges in eating more food than required for the body. Even tigers or lions take as much as required to satisfy hunger. Again human beings alone try to satisfy their palate rather than restricting the food intake as required for the sustenance of the body. That is why other species have no obesity problem.

Rachael Heller & Richard Heller:

"No matter what plan the successful dieters follow, their ability to stay focused on themselves, their needs, and their preferences, along with their ability to give up trying to please other people make all the difference in the world."

Controlling weight is directly related to controlling diet and doing regular exercise. The diet has to be controlled quantitatively as well as qualitatively. Generally most of us indulge in satisfying the palate which has to be avoided. Restraining the palate is not a one time effort, it has to become part of our life.

A strict routine and moderate diet will keep away obesity.

Moods play an important part in overeating. If we are under stress, to compensate the bad mood we tend to take more food.

As age increases, the capacity of a person to exercise or digest food diminishes. But due to habit formed for years, he tends to take the same quantum of diet as he is used to It is, therefore, necessary to closely monitor increase in weight and accordingly reduce the quantum of diet or alternatively make necessary changes in the type of food so that the overall calories are regulated.

Whenever weight is reduced, the body tries to restore it to its original level in a short period of time. We should, therefore, make the reduced weight as a reference level and hold on to it by way of managing diet and exercise.

Bramhacharya or celibacy

Sex is one area which requires to be guided by ethics and as per ethics, there is no place for indulgence in sex before marriage and after marriage it has to be done with the spouse only. Else it is promiscuity and unethical.

Mahatma Gandhi, contrary to the general perception, strongly believed that sex is not a natural physiological necessity and that there is no purpose for indulging in sex other than for creating progeny. He was opposed to the idea of indulging in sex to satisfy lust. In Hindu scriptures, a lot of importance is attached to *bramhacharya* particularly during the formative period of one's life.

The motive for sex is important while indulging in sex. Indulgence in sex is draining away on each occasion vital energy, which tantamounts to paying a heavy cost for obtaining fleeting pleasure. Therefore, both partners have to consider whether sex is desirable or not and exercise utmost restraint.

It is most unfortunate that the present society is falling prey to the vested interests of the media which is systematically directed towards corrupting the minds of the people especially youth. The easy availability of contraceptives has given a boost to permissiveness as there is no fear of the consequences of indulgence. But those who indulge forget the long term effects of such indulgence.

Health maintenance and age

There are reports of a few old people living up to the age of 113-116 years. Although a lot of research is being done to find out how to totally prevent the aging process, there has not been success in this area as yet. However, between the two, namely, adding years to the life and life to the years, more important is adding life to the years, which means quality of life should have preference over living longer.

While in general it is observed that age has a wearing down effect on human beings, we also observe some people almost retaining their youth-like physical and mental faculties in their sixties or even seventies and beyond. The things that enabled them to retain these qualities are found to be that they are regular in their habits and follow natural laws of health such as proper diet, exercise, rest & recreation and a positive mental attitude. Further, the wellbeing of a man is largely affected by the emotional aspect. They seem to have taken care of this particular aspect by the practice of positive thinking and avoiding draining of energy by negative thinking such as by fear, anger, obsession, attachment, guilt, hatred, anxiety and worry.

When a person becomes old he has already gone through many pleasant as well as unpleasant situations. Throughout life he has endured pain many times. In old age due to diminishing strength and sometimes due to absence of adequate social support, he has to be prepared for facing further problems on these fronts. Having done all that is necessary for remedying the situation, if there is no cure, endurance (both mental and physical) is one quality that helps. There is a saying, "What can not be cured has to be endured." We can pray to God for giving us the necessary strength to endure it.

Good health is the foundation for the development of personality. Our physical wellbeing depends upon how much care we take about following natural laws of health such as proper diet, exercise, rest & recreation and a positive mental attitude toward life and work. Our emphasis has to be on preventive health care rather than depending upon medical treatment for cure. The proverb, "A stitch in time saves nine" explains this concept in a better way. In this book an endeavor has been made to offer specific natural solutions to the problems being faced by humanity.

The commonest of the serious problems is managing stress and obesity. Stress is the single most cause for maximum ailments in the world. Especially heart problem which is the foremost killer disease, is directly related to stress. Coping with stressors has now become the major preoccupation of a human being. Similarly, obesity has also become a major problem.

As mentioned earlier, the root cause of most of the health problems is disregarding the natural laws of health.

"Education does not mean merely a knowledge of letters but it means character-building, a knowledge of duty."

Mahatma Gandhi

FIVE
The Competent You

Knowledge is power

Leave aside university education, one out of every four persons in India is illiterate. This is the status more than 60 years after the country became an independent republic. In the past one could manage with some education or even without education because agriculture was the main profession and one did not require education to do agriculture. However there is no way to succeed in to-day's competitive world without having proper education.

It is to be noted with satisfaction that there is a greater realization among people about the importance of education and a wave of education is sweeping across the country. There is an earnest effort even in poor families to send children to school even though they find difficulty in making both ends meet. Two bills aiming to provide free and compulsory education to children in the age group of 6 to 14 as well as right to education have been passed by Parliament.

The objective of education is beyond literacy. It is to offer us a structured learning programme which enables us to see any problem in life in the true perspective. Many people in later life regret that they did not pay attention to education in their young age and if they had done so they would have been much better off. Since education is the foundation on which the superstructure of later life rests, one should try to utilize all options to get as much education as possible during the formative age.

We are born with certain natural abilities. These grow with age. We should be open to learn new things. Education adds to the ability of a person not only to earn a livelihood but also acquire knowledge. If one has a degree in mechanical engineering and a new factory in the vicinity is looking for young graduates, you could be the one in hot demand. With the advent of high technology, science and technical subjects have assumed great importance. Information Technology is relatively a new field requiring a large number of persons with knowledge of computers. Persons having knowledge in the IT field are in hot demand. Simply put knowledge is power.

Knowledge → power

We have passed through the Stone Age, hunter's age, agriculture age, manufacturing age, and now we are passing through the knowledge age. Thus we have moved from predominantly physical attainments to physical plus mental attainments. It is very essential to gain enough knowledge to live in the present times. Accumulation of knowledge is a continuous process. We require to continuously up date our knowledge as the changes in our systems of work are taking place so quickly. Old technology is getting obsolete quickly and a new one is taking its place.

Presently significant improvement has taken place in pre-school education. More creative methods like learning drawing, painting, music, art and craft are introduced. There is also stress on pictorial presentation rather than cramming. As against pre-school education, school education is oriented more toward passing examinations. No stress is laid on developing clear concepts. This has resulted in gaining only superficial knowledge. In practical life this knowledge is hardly helpful.

Even before a child goes to school or even during schooling, learning at home makes a huge difference. Children are very keen in their perception and they always perceive their parents as role models. The parents have therefore to set the example if they wish their children to pick up good habits. For example, if a father has a smoking habit, it is very difficult to prevent the child from imitating this habit.

At home, it is easy to teach a child about cleanliness, sanitation, hygiene, and tidiness. He can also be taught about ethics i.e. character building; good behavior, truthfulness, honesty, non-injury to others etc. Parents should express love towards their children and take proper care so that they are kept away from undesirable situations. However they should avoid pampering their children. Pampering makes the child attention-seeking and such a child will find difficulty in adjusting with other children he comes in contact with.

Education at home will lay a good foundation for holistic development of the child and deriving maximum advantage from what he will be taught in school.

There are various sources of knowledge. To name a few, these are: print media- text books; guides; journals, newspapers, periodicals, reports etc.; internet, cable & satellite TV; personal discussions; symposiums, seminars and workshops. The media is using all kinds of methods to promote the sale of products, even wrong ones. There is now so much information flow around that if one is not selective one will simply get inundated by the amount of material. One has therefore to be extremely careful in selecting material which is really useful.

If wisdom is a whole, knowledge is one part of the whole. There are many who have tremendous amount of knowledge but in practice they do not know how to apply it. They get puzzled with minor problems. On the other hand, there are persons who have no knowledge but they have better insight and wisdom. It is, however, far better if there is a combination of education and wisdom.

There are some sayings like:

> Knowledge is power
> Ignorance is bliss
> Half knowledge is dangerous

Ignorance is bliss at times in as much as the person will not become a source of embarrassment or he will not embarrass anybody when he keeps silent or only listens instead of talking something irrelevant. 'Half knowledge is dangerous' is proved from the fact that many patients suffer every day at the hands of quack doctors. Similarly it is harmful to indulge in negative thinking or having misinformation. In such situations ignorance or no-knowledge is a more appropriate option.

Teachers and teaching

The method of teaching is more of a personal trait of a teacher. The teacher should help in enabling students to become self reflective rather than cramming the contents of the books. It is also a duty of the teacher to see that the minds of the students grow with their teaching as physical muscles grow with exercise. They must ensure that the students exert themselves enough for their own good rather than adopting the path of least interest in the welfare of the students.

To teach students who are normal or good at studies does not require special efforts. They are self supporting. However, there are some students who are slow at learning. The teacher has to take a sympathetic view of such students and spend more time with them so that they feel that they are part of the main stream of the education process.

In olden times, education used to be treated as a noble profession and teachers used to be respected by students as one's parents. They were respected by society too. Teachers also used to care for the welfare of the students. However, over a period of time, teaching has become for some commercial business. There is a loss of value system on the side of the teacher as well as the student and society. However, there are many sincere teachers and students respect them even now. But they are not getting the kind of respect they should get from society in general.

IT can play an important role in the field of education. For increasing the level of education, besides shortage of classrooms, textbooks and other facilities, a major factor is shortage of qualified teachers. Distance e-learning modules can do the job of teaching to a great extent. In fact children may find some of the interactive modules more interesting. The modules have also the distinct advantage of easy updating as against updating knowledge manually.

Developing skill and right mental attitude

Knowledge alone will not take us far unless we possess the necessary skill of application of the knowledge in practice. Talent is important, but a practice makes the difference between being good and being brilliant.

An equation given below showing the relationship between knowledge, skill and power represents the correct picture.

Knowledge + Skill = Power

It is not that people are born with skill. Skill can be developed. The trickiest of skills is to ride a bicycle, drive a vehicle on the road or pilot a plane. How do people learn driving skills for the first time when there is every likelihood of serious accidents in which many lives could be involved? We learn by practice.

Here again if we possess knowledge and skill but do not have the right attitude towards work, whatever power we wield on the basis of knowledge and skill will not be sustainable in the long run. Therefore, the following equation represents a more wholesome picture.

Knowledge + Skill + Right Attitude = Real Power

Learning is a continuing process

Knowledge is so vast that there is no boundary line. There are different fields and aspects in the universe. Even many lifetimes will not be sufficient to know fully about a single field or aspect. Therefore learning is a continuing process. Many of us tend to think that we know all about a particular subject. Holding such a belief is wrong and will inhibit us from making further progress in life.

Knowledge has no bounds. In order to increase our stock of knowledge and wisdom, we must have receptivity to new ideas. We should learn something new every day to add to our knowledge bank. However if side by side we utilize the knowledge it develops synergy.

Sharing of knowledge is very important. This should however be done when the sharer has acquired sufficient knowledge on the subject and the recipient is ready for receiving the knowledge. This would enable the sharer to influence and help the cause which he may consider as dear to him. One peculiar thing with sharing of knowledge is that the knowledge of the sharer increases by sharing. During the process of teaching others, one learns something new from others.

In the present context, education has assumed highest importance because the progress of a person in later life is much dependent on his educational qualification. Education is the foundation on which the superstructure of later life rests.

It becomes therefore a duty of parents to guide their wards to get educated as much as possible during their formative age. It is also the responsibility of the wards to take their studies seriously lest they regret later that they did not do enough to educate themselves at the right time. Fortunately there is now more awareness in parents as well as wards than ever about the importance of education. However education is only a first step for the progress of a person. The academic education has to be backed up by learning skills and the right mental attitude to succeed in life. Such a combination provides the synergy much required now-a-days to succeed in life.

"The deepest principle in human nature is the craving to be appreciated."

William James

SIX
Relationships

Healthy Interpersonal Relationship

Man is a social animal. Of all the subjects in the world, the most complex is the knowledge of human nature. The working of the human brain is still largely a mystery. Although a lot of research has taken place in this field, very little is known. There are certain fundamental laws which govern the universe and the same applies to its habitants as well. It is to our benefit if we know these laws. However, the situational and personal differences add to the complexities of human nature.

In an organization or a family, in politics or governance or for that matter in any field, we have to deal with people. Even machines like computers are ultimately handled by people.

Thus living in this world is synonymous with working with people. Life becomes easier for those who find it easy to work with people. We find one commonality in the people who are at the helm of affairs. They have a clearer understanding of what determines human behaviour.

Need for good interpersonal relationship

Just as many strands make a strong rope, it is good to have a group of people interacting and working as one team.

The efforts of a team of persons will always be more powerful and as a team they will be able to achieve greater things in comparison with efforts of a single man. However, to get desired results, good interpersonal relationship is the prerequisite. This is visible in sports which involve team work.

Dependency is the characteristic of a child while interdependency is the characteristic of adults. In this paradigm there are persons who can be termed as independent. Independent persons will work in a purely individualistic way. They will derive strength from their ego or inner self.

If there is any law which governs interpersonal relationship, it is a law of reciprocity. Simply put, it means whatever way we behave with others, others will most likely behave with us in the same fashion. The best example of this law can be found in the manner of relationship between neighbours. If a person is helpful to his neighbour at the time of need, it is quite certain that his neighbour will also help this person when he is in difficulty.

Perceptions and beliefs

Perception of a situation will vary from person to person. Every person has his own idea as to how things are and how they should be. Even when facts remain the same, interpretation of the facts differs.

One painter put up his painting asking the viewers to mark the places where the painting looks good so that he retains that style in future. At the end, the painting was filled with right marks. On another occasion, he shows a similar painting asking the viewers to put cross marks where the painting does not look good so that he avoids that style in future. Interestingly at the end, the painting was full with cross marks. Obviously there were as many right markers as cross markers. This only highlights the fact that perceptions differ from person to person.

Whether we agree or not we should respect the other person's perception otherwise that person is bound to become our adversary. After all we should recognize the fact that his perception is based upon his thoughts, experiences and judgment of the matter as much as our perception is based upon our thoughts, experiences and judgment. Instead of saying he is wrong, a better way will be to say, "I may be wrong but I feel........" In this case there are good chances of appreciation of our perception in proper perspective and even if the person does not agree, surely he will not become our adversary.

When we find that our perception is wrong, rather than being rigid, we should be ready to accept the reality irrespective of the fact that it did not occur to us at the right time. If we don't it shows weakness on our part. On the other hand it shows real strength and character on our part when we admit our mistake and apologize for it. Admitting a mistake puts us immediately on a much higher pedestal in the eyes of others.

Every human being, being unique in personality, has his own perception about any subject. Even twins could have different perceptions. Members of one family often differ widely in perception of any situation.

Beliefs are formed out of our social and cultural ethos and our own life's experiences. In this context, the experiences in early childhood take deeper roots as compared to later periods of life. If parents do not have a good relationship with each other, the child is likely to be insecure. The child considers his parents as role models and as people who can be trusted.

Key to a healthy interpersonal relationship

The family represents a laboratory in which the art of relationship between the members of the family is tested. It gives unique training to its members for interacting with the outside world. The family environment has great influence on the personal advancement of each family member.

The primary responsibility of creating a congenial environment falls directly on the head of the family (*karta*) and his spouse (house lady). The responsibility of other members comes next. In this context, the nature of the relationship between husband and wife sets the example for others and therefore plays a crucial role in developing a harmonious relationship within the family.

The relationship between husband and wife should reflect the spirit of partnership. If the family is to grow happily, the responsibility for this lies on both.

There are times when one of the partners may be busy with certain things. In such situations it is better if the other partner cooperates in shouldering the family responsibility. It is necessary that both of them should jointly work out how they can share the responsibilities rather than expecting fairness only from the partner.

As human beings, both husband and wife tend to have their own perceptions. However, when these perceptions differ very widely, conflicts are generated. As these conflicts get piled up over a period of time, the relationship gets sour, sometimes beyond repair. The reversing of roles for a while will give a different perspective to both the spouses. Both should address the question; what each of them needs to do to make life better.

A positive mental attitude is the foundation stone for good interpersonal relationship. People with a positive mental attitude attract each other and develop friendship when they come in contact. When two persons with positive mental attitude come together, the strength of both increases. On the other hand people would like to avoid those who have a negative mental attitude. In this busy world nobody would like to fritter away their time and energy in coping with people with a negative mental attitude.

Trustworthiness is an essential feature of interpersonal relationship. Trustworthiness flows from character. Trustworthiness is the foundation on which the building of interpersonal relationship rests. Nobody would like to work with an unreliable person. Trustworthiness binds the members of a family, organization or society just as cement binds together the bricks of the building. Where there is trustworthiness, one is sure about getting one's worth for the trust put in by one. On the other hand, once mistrust develops between persons, the goodness in their interpersonal relationship gets affected.

Trustworthiness and commitments go together. Commitments once made should be honoured. Commitments should be made only after careful consideration.

A healthy interrelationship calls for the exercise of a number of active efforts on the part of individuals dealing with each other. Empathy, understanding, attentiveness and consideration for other, a genuine feeling of involvement in others' happiness, a charitable disposition and inclination to help others–these are some of the factors that go a long way in strengthening the bonds between individuals. Ultimately they help in creating a network of relationships in a society.

Empathy is ability to identify with a person or object. It reflects our concern for the welfare of the other person. There are many people who have physical disabilities. There are others who are very poor. There are people who are struggling to overcome personal tragedies. All such people need a helping hand. If we show our empathy with them at such times, it helps to boost their morale. Let us not forget that there could be a time when we could be in difficulty. We all wish others should understand our point of view. It is necessary to understand others' points of view first. This makes for a congenial relationship.

On many occasions when somebody is talking to us, although we pretend that we are listening to him, our thoughts are roaming somewhere else. If the other person happens to notice it, he is bound to feel slighted. If we wish people to like us it is important that we genuinely pay attention to what others are saying to us.

Many of us are miserly in expressing our love, may be love towards a child, spouse or a friend. Why are we not generous about it when we don't lose anything and there is everything to gain by expressing it?

To develop and carry forward good interpersonal relationship, it is necessary to continue to give timely positive strokes to the person with whom we wish to develop a relationship.

We all hold certain beliefs and have some values dear to us. In this context whenever we interact with others, there should be some consistency in our behaviour which will reflect our values. Those with whom we often interact form a certain image of us over a period of time. They would expect that our behaviour will be in line with that image.

We become dependent on other people's perception about ourselves. If we concentrate on developing our ability to perform well, we need not be unhappy if other people are also performing well. That man is great who derives happiness in finding other people happy or smiles when he sees other people smiling.

Nothing can be so pleasant to a person than hearing his own name when addressed by another person. If we recognize the person we met earlier and call him by name, that person feels elated. On the other hand, many a misunderstanding develops when we fail to recognize or remember names of people we met earlier. Remembering names is one of the most outstanding qualities in interpersonal relationship and achieving success in life.

A pleasant expression on the face helps one get along well in life. When we wish something to be done, it helps if we willfully create a bond with those whom we deal with. Simply wishing him, asking about his welfare helps create a bond. In the field of sales and marketing, a pleasant expression has become one of the most important criteria. How well it will be if the same thing happens in other fields as well.

Many people find it interesting to offer advice to others whether others want it or not. A person who himself has not imbibed the quality and qualification he preaches has no business to advise others. Such advice will lack authenticity. Gandhiji became popular with the masses because he was himself practicing what he was propagating.

To continue with the qualities enumerated for a healthy inter relationship, a few more points can be stressed.

One should aim at presenting an agreeable and pleasant relationship with people one deals with. But one should not be taken advantage of. Parting of ways should also be done in an equally pleasant manner. Likewise, it should be possible to agree to disagree without overreaction.

A change of job or place will lead to the formation of new relationships. One should learn to broaden one's view of life with such changes. In life there are many situations which call for different kinds of responses. Some people may act in order to hurt you and derive satisfaction if you are hurt. If your response does not show this such satisfaction cannot be achieved. Trying to reason with such individuals would be a good way to tackle them.

When somebody is interacting with another there are three ways of responding. One is responding in a positive mode, the second is a neutral mode and the third one is the negative mode. Some management experts call the first one as responsive and the third one as reactive. The responsive mode is associated with rationality, whereas the reactive mode is associated with disproportionate emotions. While responsive and reactive modes are two ends of a paradigm, it is not unusual to find the response in a combination of two modes. Positive response reflects a feeling of love, whereas negative response reflects a feeling of disregard for the other person.

Though we don't realize it, words are very powerful. We express our thoughts in them. Even the tone of the word spoken changes according to how intensely we feel about an event. Words make or break relationships. Therefore, we should speak words which are appropriate in a situation.

It is easy as well as common to find a weakness in the other person, more so if that person is familiar. In everybody's life, the most familiar person is a life partner: a wife or husband. The husband may find some fault in his wife and feed himself with that thought day in and day out. After some time it becomes his second nature. In such a situation even her other merits pass off unnoticed by him. Instead of getting obsessed by such a thought, he should try to improve his own self which could motivate her as well to change. Before we expect improvement in others' behaviour, we should ourselves set the example.

Help and service to needy

Life is a process of evolution. We notice that if we casually ask a small child to part with a thing given to him by the elders at home or any belonging of his home, he would not like to part with it. This nature manifests itself deeper when he grows up, the only difference being that in grown up people, the self interest will be well cloaked with seeming rationality. However wisdom should dawn upon grown up persons to shed this attribute of selfishness for their own sake and work for the larger interest of the society as they can afford it. The moot point is if everybody in the society works with selfishness, the very foundation of society, which requires contribution from its members for its survival, will be affected adversely.

As a human being service should come naturally to us to help the needy. We should become genuinely interested in others before we expect others to get interested in us. Spontaneous desire to sympathize and provide service to others who need it is an admirable quality. Providing help to others may create some inconvenience to us. But we have to keep in mind that at some other time we may be in difficulty and require others' help.

Providing service to the underserved stands on a different footing altogether. Some are born in poor and disadvantaged families. They deserve better priority. People are normally quite busy in giving and taking help and such persons may belong to a well off category. They have no idea that they are missing the most important point i.e. underserved persons deserve the help most. We must give priority to make a difference to the lives of the underserved. A gesture of generosity by us can bring immense joy to their lives.

Charity is giving voluntarily to those in need. Though the word is well meaning, it is being utilized in desirable as well as undesirable ways by the providers of charity as well as those who accept charity. If the transaction takes place at the humanistic level where both provider and receiver maintain their self-worth, such charity is desirable. However, if the transaction takes place at the level of the ego i.e. when the provider feels himself proud as he is giving charity and the receiver feels loss of his self-worth, this kind of charity is a misnomer for the word and undesirable.

There are many institutions which with the resources they have are doing well to serve the underserved and a number of service motivated people join such institutions. On the other hand there are many organizations which are otherwise. Gandhiji has suggested a better way of helping the underserved. Instead of giving charity like money, poor should be enabled to get work (for which they are paid) so that they can maintain themselves and their families with dignity.

Assistance required in times of illness or emergency should be seen in a totally different perspective. In that case we have to ignore our comforts or priorities and provide help to the needy. In this context I remember a person named S. C. Aggrawal whose old mother went into coma. She remained in coma for several years. Aggrawal did bother about his career but took a lighter job so that he could take care of his mother. He fed his mother and cleaned her himself. He did not leave these things even to his wife. Blessed are such sons to their mothers.

Having said human beings are interdependent, we should enjoy doing service to others as well as accept service from others. Since there is a hidden joy in giving service to others, the other person also gets similar joy in giving service to us. Therefore, why deny him enjoying giving service to us?

Acceptance of service should invariably be accompanied by expression of gratitude. There are times when others provide service to us and we don't even take notice of it. In such cases the service provider gets disheartened and he is less likely to provide the service next time as willingly as before.

Man is a social animal. One may be in any field of activity, but one will have to deal with people. Even machines are to be operated by human beings only. As such they are not replacements for human beings. Thus, living in this world is closely linked to working with people. Since a person can not meet his full requirement by himself and he has to depend on others for some need or the other, life becomes interdependent. It is easier for those who are good at developing sound interpersonal relationships to become successful in life.

Trustworthiness, good behavior, trying to understand others' points of view, helping the needy are some of the qualities which enable a person to develop good interpersonal relationship.

"Lost wealth may be replaced by industry, lost knowledge by study, lost health by temperance or medicine, but lost time is gone forever."

Samuel Smiles

"Realize that now, in this moment of time, you are creating your next moment. That is what's real."

Sarah Paddison

SEVEN
Time Management

How much time is really with us?

The time available in life is not unlimited. The average span of life varies from country to country. While it is 65 in India, in some developed countries it is 77. With increasing awareness about maintaining physical fitness and phenomenal improvement in medical facilities especially in urban areas, life span is improving. So in the not too distant future we can assume 80 years as the average life span.

Let us make some assumptions based upon our working conditions:

1. Let us assume we spend about three weeks in a year toward leave from the work place as well as rest during illness. We will also assume five days a week as a working period. We thus get 365-21-104 (i.e. 2x52) = 240 days as the working days in a year.
2. Let's assume average working hours as eight hours per day. Generally effective utilization of time is less than half and the rest goes in handling something (like meetings, discussions, seminars, presentations, reports, cell phone calls etc.) which is not core work. Thus we get 960 (i.e. 240x4) hours in a year.
3. Leaving out the initial life span of 25 years towards education and the last five years towards old age problems, we get a period of 50 years as a productive life span
4. We thus get a period of 48,000 (i.e. 960x50) hours. As a percentage of the total lifespan of (80x365x24=) 700,800 hours, effective working time (48,000/700,800) is just below seven percent.

Thus although we may be thinking that we are busy in our profession, effective time spent in the profession is below seven percent of the total time available to us.

Considering the earth's existence for millions of years, a lifespan of 80 years is just a small one. Time once past cannot be brought back unless we can cross the limit of the speed of light. Life is how one has spent time throughout a lifetime. There is a religious belief that after death a count is taken of the good and evil deeds one has done during one's lifetime and depending upon the sum total, one goes to heaven or hell. Those who believe in reincarnation, believe that the deeds will determine the family in which one will take the next birth.

Whatever it is, if one wishes to achieve something worthwhile and enjoy life, one can ill afford to waste time on anything which is not useful. Of course human beings require time for rest and recreation to repair the physical body just as machines are stopped at intervals for repair and maintenance. Time is money. When any project takes more time than normal, its original cost gets escalated. Likewise in personal life, we experience cost escalation when we receive hefty telephone bills for a long talk.

There is no better method of time management than planning activities in advance.

Time is confidence. When we experience our goals getting accomplished on time as planned, we get a feeling of happiness along with a feeling of confidence. This feeling of confidence encourages us to set higher goals.

Time as a resource for success

Among all resources, time is the most precious. Time has become such an important subject that in management jargon it is addressed as time management. However we can't manage time in the sense that it is simply not within our control as the clock goes on ticking all the time even if you hold the pendulum.

We have to manage our activities within the time available. We should plan our activities for the day in advance. They should be listed according to priority which will be generally guided by their value and urgency.

I took to writing for my first book, *Integrated Approach to Rural Development* in 2003. It took me full two years to complete the book. I had to work not only for most part of the day but even late hours during the night. During this period, not only did my health deteriorate but I could pay little or no attention to my wife who was managing the home. Obviously our interpersonal relationship was at its lowest ebb.

In retrospect I feel I could have done better by balancing time between writing and sharing responsibility at home. From the prefaces of writers of several books, I find other writers too went through similar experiences.

We do not always use our time judiciously. Most of us invest our time on unnecessary details and in the process we lose sight of some important aspects. We waste time on non-issues and in the process gloss over issues of substance.

The famous old rule of 80: 20 states that 80 percent of our time is spent for 20 per cent of activities. We can find out for ourselves as to how we are spending time by logging, for one week, time that we planned to spend and the time actually spent for various activities. This would give us an idea as to the areas in which we have overspent time.

There is no point in burdening ourselves with too many activities if we are not able to execute them properly without overstraining ourselves. Constant burdening ourselves causes exhaustion. While it is our duty to give time to others who genuinely need it, we should learn to politely say no to people for whom it is just not possible to spare the time.

The working of the universe is governed by the principle of two dimensions, namely, time and space. Presently the average life span of a human being is below 80 years. As mentioned earlier effective utilization of time is around 7 percent. The rest is spent in sleep, routine personal chores, and incidental to profession. When we have to do a number of tasks in a day or over a certain period, the best way is to rearrange them in terms of importance and urgency. It should not matter if certain things are left out in the process as long as prioritization has been done wisely.

When we have too many tasks to do, we must do first things first. We should develop a clear sense of our priorities and focus our attention to accomplish them.

Priority is different from undertaking a venture. When we have limitation of capability, it is always advisable to start with a small venture. With success in a small venture we can build our capability to undertake bigger and bigger ventures.

We must first take care of one of our activities which matters most. Earlier I used to start with reading the newspaper, checking e-mails, surfing on the internet or finding stock market trends. This used to consume more time and energy with little in return. This left me with little enthusiasm for carrying out writing work. Quickly I decided to start the day with writing and now I find I am on the right track and it gives me immense satisfaction.

Delegating activities is essence of conserving energy

There are several situations and myriad activities that keep calling for our attention. We do not have unlimited time and energy at our disposal. Here comes the importance of delegating work as well as prioritizing activities.

It is not only difficult but often impossible to remember each and every activity to be done. Use the organizer a date-wise planner which is extensively used now-a-days. The organizer is the best tool for prioritization and conserving energy.

To conclude, time is the most precious resource. When we lose a moment, it is lost for ever. Since our life span is not unlimited, we have to prioritize our activities on a continuous basis. Time management is a key to one's success. While prioritizing activities we have to ensure that activities which are of personal importance to us are not overtaken by urgent activities. In this context, the use of an organizer has been found to be very helpful in planning, prioritizing and monitoring the activities on a day to day basis.

"Every human being has some spark of power by which he can create something that has not been created before."
Sri Sri Paramahansa Yogananda

"If I have made any valuable discoveries, it has been owing more to patient attention than to any other talent"
Sir Isaac Newton

EIGHT
Towards Creativity and Wisdom

How to develop creativity

Every now and then our life throws problems for which there are no routine solutions. These problems can be best solved by creativity on the part of those engaged with the work. Various inventions which have taken place so far are the products of man's creativity.

The environment in which we work is ever changing. In an effort to make life easier, there is a constant effort to produce things that give greater comfort.

The entire space programme is a living example of the creativity of man. To get over the gravitational pull of earth and then station a vehicle in space or man landing on a different planet are all such feats which could not have been possible without creativity on the part of human beings.

Creativity is a natural ability. We are all born with this quality. According to estimates, 97 percent of children between the ages of nine months and five years are rated as creative. However, by the fag end of their academic education phase (around the age of 25 years), only 7 percent remain creative. What could be the cause for such steep diminishing of the numbers? This happens because during their formal education phase they are subjected to psychological pressure to conform to an ethos existing around them. This level further goes down with increasing age.

Given the right environment and the personal effort almost 97 percent could remain creative. Creativity can be tapped at any time. As any other quality, creativity is subject to disuse meaning thereby that the less we use creativity the more we lose it.

We have been consciously or unconsciously doing new things and doing things differently from our early childhood. We witness how creative minded people constantly find new ways to deal with intricate problems. Changing from tedious and slow manual working to easier and fast working on computers is just an example. Therefore we should try to keep such a wonderful process of reinventing ourselves continuing throughout our life and even in old age.

There are certain prerequisites for the expression of creativity, the foremost being complete freedom in doing work. Too much regulatory pressure will not be conducive for anyone to express his creativity. On the other hand, if the person finds the work meaningful and it is left to him how it has to be done, he will use his creativity to solve any difficult problem that will be encountered in doing the work. Experience shows setting important guidelines works better than creating a regulatory mechanism.

Creativity has no restriction like a particular field of activity. First of all we should understand that no job is beneath us. Every activity is important. It does not matter who does it. Creativity can be applied to any field of activity. Of course, by this we don't mean there is creativity in every aspect i.e. even in evil acts. This will be called destructivity. Creativity enables positive outcomes.

Fields of activity for creativity can be small or big and the nature of activity can be anything like gardening, cooking, cleaning, sewing, painting, playing music, writing and so on. It depends upon how interesting we make that activity.

Often in the complex world of today we look for short-term gains and in the process ignore a big loss that is likely to happen in the long run. As we grow in age we increase our knowledge and experience. We should utilize all available knowledge and experience to get a larger perspective of life. Any happening that takes place should be seen against that perspective so that our efforts are concentrated on achieving our goals rather than frittering away our energy on trivial things. It is rightly said, "We should try to win the game rather than a point."

Creativity requires one to be wholly involved in the work. This is possible only when the work itself is interesting to the person concerned. It requires initiative on the part of a person to try new ways of doing things. He may make mistakes in the process, but he should learn from the mistakes, rectify them and proceed ahead. It is not possible to achieve anything great with a half hearted approach.

Doing things differently is always looked upon with skepticism. It also involves a certain amount of risk. When one tries to do things differently, others may be skeptical about the correctness of one's actions but if the results are favorable, others would appreciate doing things differently.

Creativity being a new way of doing things involves some amount of risk. The train of thoughts in creativity is different from the conventional thoughts veering round maintaining a status quo. The person who is doing creative work as well as others concerned should be ready for taking risks.

Fear arises when we stop trusting our ability. Tenzing Norgay, succeeded in climbing Mt. Everest, because he had confidence in himself. He had a dream; he had no fear of failure. Only those who shed fear can achieve something great. However this does not suggest that we should risk our life in the process.

We should try to do things as best as possible but we should not be after perfection. In doing one thing perfectly, we may miss many other things. Some people in trying to attain perfection make not only their life miserable but they also make others' lives difficult. These people develop high expectations and when the expectations are not fulfilled they become unhappy. It is therefore better to redefine perfection as "doing things as best as possible."

Creativity has no age bar. Although this quality is found in abundance in children, some older persons as well display it. Usually during adulthood we get too engrossed in doing mundane activities which are mostly related to providing for day to day requirements. During this phase our creative talent, other than related to work in hand, generally remains dormant. In this context post-retirement time provides a unique opportunity to express our hidden talent.

Having gone through varied, good as well as bad, experiences throughout one's life, one would and should be interested to see good things happen during the last lap of one's journey. This is also a time to reflect on what we have achieved in life so as to be aware of what we are leaving behind as our legacy for the younger generation.

How to develop intelligence

According to Dr. C. George Boeree of Shippenburg University, intelligence is a person's capacity to (1) acquire knowledge (i.e. learn and understand), (2) apply knowledge (solve problems), and (3) engage in abstract reasoning. It is the power of one's intellect, and as such is clearly a very important aspect of one's overall well being.

Intelligence also means quickness of understanding and thus ability to comprehend. Every human being is endowed with intelligence in lesser or higher degree. Intelligence helps us to respond quickly to any situation. Psychologists have attempted to measure it for well over a century and the measure is named as Intelligence Quotient (IQ). There are several methods to measure IQ and several factors go into the measurement of IQ.

Though generally believed to be immutable, recent research suggests that certain mental activities can change the brain's raw ability to process information, leading to the conclusion that intelligence can be altered or changed over time. Thus like any other quality, intelligence can also be developed. When we start using intelligence, more neurons get activated; more connections and interconnections take place in the brain thus increasing the level of thinking and in turn intelligence. A person may be intelligent in securing good grades in school but if he does not apply his intelligence in acting in real life situations, theoretical intelligence is of no use. Intelligence alone does not take us far. Together with intelligence we require experience in a particular field of activity to become successful in that field.

Intelligence has its limitations. Unless it is backed by power of discrimination, intelligence alone will not be able to help us in all situations.

Intelligence tempered with experience leads us to wisdom and wisdom helps us to solve any problem in life. Thus there is a clear distinction between intelligence and wisdom.

How to develop wisdom

Wisdom is seen in the young as well as the old. As any person with more experience and age is generally expected to become wiser, we should try to seek guidance from them. However there is no direct relationship between wisdom and experience or age, because one may or may not have ability or will to draw correct inferences from experiences. That is why many experienced and old people are also found committing mistakes. On the other hand many young people and even children are found to possess wisdom which surpasses learned adults and old people. Sri Vivekananda, Sri Paramahansa Yogananda as well as many saints and others displayed wisdom from an early age.

Wisdom can be developed by being inwardly quiet, doing meditation, praying, reading inspiring literature and doing constructive work. We should associate with such persons who we think have made progress on the spiritual path.

Knowledge can be either theoretical or practical. Although both are assets, practical knowledge is more desirable. Theoretical knowledge can be insufficient or even half knowledge and as such in some situations can be dangerous. Knowledge which supports right actions becomes a source of wisdom. But when knowledge is used to defeat the right purpose, it becomes a bad tool. In practical life we find many people knowing well that what they are arguing about is wrong, still plead for it with all (so called) knowledge at their command.

Awareness which is a basis for knowledge helps us to live in the present. But heightened awareness helps us to live with wisdom.

Before Newton everybody had seen fruits falling down from trees. However Newton was the first one to feel curiosity about this phenomenon which led to the great discovery of gravity of the earth. Newton found this because he paid patient attention to the phenomenon. We miss many opportunities in life because we do not pay attention when they are right before us.

Knowledge and wisdom cannot be easily acquired if bias enters one's perceptions and beliefs. In interpersonal relationships it is usual to notice biases. It is not uncommon even in families. Bias is the main cause for bad interpersonal relationship. Therefore we should always check whether our belief is based on current facts about the situation or not.

Maturity is a function of wisdom rather than age or knowledge. Although long experience and wide knowledge are helpful in attaining maturity, these factors may not be of any help if the person who has these does not know how to use them wisely. Humility and a rational approach are more useful than an ego and arrogance.

How to develop power of judgment

Judgment is a critical faculty for taking right decisions. In day to day life one has to constantly decide several matters, some important and some routine. If things go wrong on routine matters, it is not so bad. However, if things go wrong on important matters, the consequences may be high. Good power of judgment is most essential to achieve success in life. Good judgment requires developing good concentration.

Emotions affect our power of judgment. Say if one is attached emotionally with agriculture, it is difficult to wean him away from that occupation and expect him to take up a factory job even though the latter may offer a lucrative salary. Similarly holding irrational beliefs affect power of judgment. Keeping one's mental equilibrium is a basic requirement to improve our power of judgment. Thus even in the worst circumstances we should not lose peace of mind.

How to develop decision making power

Goals are only intentions and unless they are translated into actions they have no value. Although we may take time to consider pros and cons before any decision is taken, the whole process should not lead to procrastination. Decisions should be taken when our mind is calm and cool. It helps to step back mentally from the scene i.e. to take a short break from the process, think coolly about the vexed problems. The solution will then come easily.

Ambivalence or failing to make choices will keep us away from success. If there is no choice but to decide, one should decide based on what facts could be made available.

The actions of a man should be based upon sound logic rather than instinctive action. Every human being is required to take decisions when a situation arises. There are two types of decisions, one is reversible and the other is irreversible. Here we are using the words reversible and irreversible and their meaning in relative terms, simultaneously keeping in mind that many of the decisions may not be completely reversible or completely irreversible. We need to be very careful about the decisions which are irreversible. Most of our routine actions and for that matter decisions depend upon our intuition. The results in such cases are not very significant. However for deciding on important matters, it becomes necessary to take into account various aspects. Some of the steps which are helpful in deciding important matters are: the collection of relevant information or facts; avoidance of emotions playing a predominant part; and what our sixth sense or intuition says.

The decisions which are predominantly based upon emotions may be found to be wrong later as the context in which the decisions were taken may subsequently undergo radical change.

Whenever we take a decision, we must be responsible for its consequences too. We should not blame others if our decisions lead to failures.

Ordinarily we are in a position to take decisions based on available facts. However, there are situations when our inner voice or intuition says we should do something which is different from the logic. The power of intuition transcends logic. On many occasions we regret we did not pay heed to our intuition while deciding issues. Can intuition be developed? The real issue does not seem to be development of intuition as much as the clarity of the intuition. This clarity would depend upon how much qualitative attention we pay to understand the intuition. Those who are dedicated to the spiritual field believe that meditation, which involves concentration, helps in developing intuition.

There are occasions when we are in a dilemma about what action should be taken in a specific situation. In such a predicament, it helps to find out what our mentor or Guru would have done if he would have faced the same situation. For some, the mentor may be a personalized one, whom we call as Guru (living or not living), and for some, mentor may be religious beliefs. It is believed that those who have faith in a mentor or Guru get constant guidance in such matters.

While basic features resemble each other every human being is unique and endowed with a few distinct good qualities. Creativity, intelligence and wisdom fall into this category. It should be our endeavor to cultivate, develop and give expression to these very qualities so as to make our best contribution to society and leave a legacy behind us. The long term goal or purpose can be developed on the basis of our aptitude which is a derivative of our unique qualities. As far as a short term goal is concerned, it will depend upon the nature of the assignment we are engaged in and our day to day priorities. The quantum of success in life is directly related to how much of our short term goals are in alignment with the long term goals/purposes and how far we are steadfast in our resolve to attain them.

"Few of us can do great things, but all of us can do small things with great love."

Mother Teresa

NINE
Realising Potential

Genesis of infinite potential

Psychologists earlier propounded a theory that the genes and the life during the first two years of a baby determine the future of a person. A lot of emphasis was placed on the person's mental make up developed during early childhood. This theory is undergoing a change. It is now increasingly believed that although childhood experiences do profoundly impact shaping a personality, with efforts every human being can change and acquire a different personality and accordingly potential. The new concept gives hope especially to those whose childhood was troublesome or who went through traumatic experiences during their childhood.

The potential of a human being needed varies with the circumstances he is placed in. In a broader context, once upon a time, physical strength, courage and skill were prized because man had to constantly fight physically with the surroundings and his enemy. He was more preoccupied with protecting himself from wild beasts. Later on he was preoccupied with agriculture which required physical work. Today in adulthood the qualities needed are: a healthy body, intelligence, judgment, readiness to accept new ideas etc.

Imagine what will happen if we are living in rigid social structures, society driven by traditions and individuals without youthful energies. We would lose whatever skill or talent we possess as a result of disuse, just as iron gets rusted quickly if not used. Such a society sooner or later is bound to fail because it will not be in a position to keep pace with more advanced ones.

Globalization in trade and commerce has made national boundaries thinner and new challenges thrown by the process of globalization require the potential of an individual to be stretched to a great extent.

We have more natural potential than we think and use. But most of it remains dormant in our body. It waits for a catalyst to attain the full blown size, just as a seed waits for a contact with earth and water to become a plant. It is said that we use not more than 15 per cent of our brain capacity. The remaining 85 per cent is untapped. There is good news that more and more people have now started believing 'We become what we think'. Negative thinking, depression etc. contribute to a large extent toward limitation of our capacity.

About physical capacity, we put a limitation on ourselves by disregarding the natural laws of health and thus often falling ill. By following natural laws of health and exercise, we can improve our physical capacity to a great extent. To sum up, to succeed in life we require enough combined physical and mental strength and emotional maturity.

We should be aware of our real limitations as human beings. In terms of time and space matrix, we have a limitation of lifespan and a human being can be only at one place at a time (not omnipresent as God). But for these two limitations and their effect, there is no other limitation which is non-negotiable. We have to just think if the thing we want in life is worth the effort or not, otherwise with proper efforts generally we can have it.

As human beings we have tremendous potential. Before the invention of planes, everybody thought only birds could fly. Who thought in the nineteenth century that someday human beings will be walking on the moon? We have far more potential than we think we have. We have to discover it and use it for betterment of our lives.

How to know our real potential

When we think about increasing our potential or capacity to perform or do some work, we must first know our capacity. There are variations on the higher as well as lower side in assuming what is one's capacity. It means in our mind we usually tend to overestimate or underestimate our capacity. The underestimation of capacity stems from a false belief of incapability, whereas overestimation stems from false optimism and overconfidence.

There are two ways of knowing our capacity. One is when our mind is peaceful we know from intuition or what we call hearing our inner voice. The second is there are some standard tests, mental as well as physical, which are said to be scientifically developed. Of late these are used for admission to institutions, new job appointments, judging periodical performance either routine or for promotions or raise in pay.

While recruiting for military service, candidates have to undergo extensive physical and psychological tests. Since training people is time consuming and expensive, the selectors would like to know for sure the real potential of the candidate prior to recruitment. The correctness of these standard tests is however questionable.

Crises bring out the uniqueness and the best within us. Crises help us realize the farthest extent of our potential.

We have seen that globalization has posed challenges for indigenous producers but in a battle for survival it has improved the quality of indigenous products.

We tend to base our beliefs on the basis of our perception about the environment and the people associated with us. Our perception could be subjective and so also our beliefs. Perception of others about our potential could also be deceptive. For example, Einstein and Thomas Edison were at some time of their schooling declared as not being bright enough to be taught. But both of them became subsequently genius scientists.

How to build our potential

The best example of a contemporary human being on earth whose will power is limitless is Stephen Hawking, the British theoretical physicist at Cambridge University.

Potential can be nurtured by concentration, hard work, tapping infinite energy from our environment and such factors.

Concentration is a prerequisite for success in any field. No worthwhile achievement is possible with a restless mind. The world consists of several fields of activities and several men who carry them out. Each activity calls for a certain degree of excellence. Only a person who concentrates fully on the activity he is engaged in succeeds.

Potential cannot be built simply by thinking about it. It is a matter of doing actual work. Work has its own value. The type of work will vary according to one's aptitude, capability and willingness to do the work. Once a certain piece of work is completed satisfactorily, the potential of the person doing the work increases correspondingly.

No work should be treated as inferior when it forms part of one's duty or it is by one's diligent choice. Once chosen, one should try to do it to the best of one's ability.

There is infinite energy in the environment around us. Sunlight and unpolluted air are the greatest sources of energy. Exposure to sunlight even for small periods during the day especially at the time of sunrise and sunset invigorates our body and mind. Even indirect light of sunrays is beneficial.

Air comprises infinite energy. However, we are unable to take full benefit of air with our normal way of breathing. We can extract tremendous benefit by *pranayam*, which is described as one of the important steps in Patanjali Yoga. Usually doing *pranayam* once in the morning and once in the evening will keep our body and mind in a state of maximum potential.

When we think in terms of enhancing our potential, we have also to take care of those factors which lead to drainage of our potential. Fear, anger, obsession, attachment, guilt, hatred, anxiety, worry etc. are the potential factors which drain our energy. These are negative qualities and the same have a highly debilitating effect on the health and mind.

Subconsciously one is always in search of a role model. The system of having a Guru has come in vogue accordingly. However, such a system is not limited to religion or religious paths alone. Such a system works very well if the field of activity chosen is subtle and the Guru is an ideal in his field.

Though exact reasons are not known, some human beings are born with certain talents. As we progress in life, these talents somehow make their way in our life. It is up to us to make full use of them. These talents enable us to attain maximum potential.

When we are struck with calamity, unprecedented power flows though our body to help to get over the crisis situation. If an earthquake strikes, some people show extraordinary powers in rescuing people. Wherefrom does this power suddenly come? The soul is the source of this power. It is getting supernatural power directly from God who is Omnipotent.

Everything in life is subject to evolution. There is a huge scope for physical and mental development by human beings. Will power, concentration, taking interest in work etc. help us to enhance our potential. The potential is put to test in crisis situations and it gets stretched to the maximum level most often without our notice.

The study of life of all great personalities shows that the work that they did throughout their lives required a unique kind of inspiration, guidance and strength. The assertion of these great personalities invariably indicates that they drew these powers from the Infinite with whom they tuned their consciousness. It is possible for us as human beings to tap the same source to enhance our potential.

"No challenge will evoke so much ability as challenging oneself."

"The art of being wise is the art of knowing what to overlook."
William James

TEN
Facing Challenges

We face challenges from conception stage

The percentages of abortions and miscarriages before delivery and the percentages of infant mortality are mind-boggling. Thus what we see on earth are the ones who could survive the most difficult challenges right from the conception stage.

Any living species in the universe survives by facing challenges thrown by the environment surrounding it. The species may be plant, bird, animal or human being. Birds and animals face problems not only from nature but also from their own species as well as human beings. Human beings face problems from nature, microbes, animals and other human beings.

The birth pangs of birds, animals or human beings are more or less on similar lines. Thus every creature on earth has to strive for survival since conception. In fact challenges start growing as we grow up.

Once we face challenges and success is achieved it cannot be presumed that we will be basking in the sun. Success in its wake will cause a ripple effect in terms of a new identity, new relationships, lifestyle changes, new resources, new responsibilities etc. These will present a new set of challenges. The point is every movement will bring in its wake new challenges and one should be mentally prepared to accept these as a part of success. Likewise there will be a new set of challenges when the person will work for achieving new goals.

Challenges are disguised opportunities

We have an inherent ability to know what is needed to face the challenge howsoever hard it may be. Even assuming we fail to succeed in certain adverse circumstances which may be beyond our control, we learn some precious lessons out of our failures. We learn new skills to cope with challenges. Challenges and conflicts are thus opportunities for our growth.

Whenever we are challenged, we feel insecure, unsettled. Although we hate insecurity in our hearts, interestingly that insecurity becomes a provider of better opportunities in our life.

Usually people tend to like assignments that follow a certain definite routine. They miss an important point that the dividends of doing challenging work are always more. It means if the work is of a challenging nature, the dividends are significant. History is replete with stories of ordinary men becoming heroes when they showed extraordinary resourcefulness and courage when they were faced with extraordinary challenges.

It is easier to swim with the current in a river. But it is quite another to swim against the current especially if the odds are: high when there is a storm. People generally take to the trodden path, a traditional approach to life situations. It is said, only dead fish swim along the current. Exploring new territory is fraught with risk. But it can be and usually is a rewarding experience. Successful people choose the path which is less traveled but they reach their destination, enjoying the thrill of the journey on the way.

How do we meet challenges

Another kind of challenge is being able to face reality. Facing reality means understanding the situation as it exists and knowing one's capacity to face it. This requires knowing one's strength as well as weakness. There is no point in accepting a challenge in a hurry for which one is not prepared. But one can always prepare to face the challenge provided efforts are made in the right direction. Man is capable of solving most intricate problems.

Mostly issues perceived to be complex have simple solutions. But it requires self confidence even to find simple solutions. Many a time we complicate simple situations and make problems more complex.

While over confidence is undesirable, self confidence is essential for a person in this competitive world. A person may have knowledge but if he is not confident of himself, he would not be able to assert himself even when he is right. Self confidence however should be accompanied by understanding how to become effective.

Challenges invoke emotional responses. It is generally seen that we get a jerk at the first sight of a challenge. Our heart gets pounding. We get emotionally charged and start feeling that it will have a devastating effect on our venture.

However, surprisingly when we have finished managing this challenge, as an afterthought we feel our first reaction to the challenge was uncalled for; it did not deserve stretching our nerves or increasing our blood pressure. Instead of helping, emotional reaction is counterproductive to meet the challenge as it lowers our morale and in turn potential to face the challenge.

The earliest man in the cave did not confine himself to the cave but he came out of it and started exploring various ways for his survival and growth. Over a period of time he established civilizations. It is thus wrong to dislike a challenge. On the other hand challenge is necessary for our growth. One's birth itself is a result of a challenge faced by one's mother. A challenge should be considered as a good chance to show our worth rather than fearing it as an adversary. A challenge acts as a stimulant for raising our potential which otherwise remains dormant. It is an opportunity in disguise. A challenge can be met by preparing ourselves in advance. The qualities -- patience, hope, self confidence, right effort etc. help us to meet the challenge.

"Goal gives us a focus for concentrating our effort to achieve it."

"Failure is a normal part of the process that can impact us positively or negatively depending on how we view it."

Charles C. Manz

ELEVEN
Setting Goals

To understand the significance of the popular saying, "Life is a journey," let us find out whether we can draw a parallel between the saying and our experience of a journey by train. For undertaking a journey by train, we have to book tickets in advance. Therefore, the destination has to be decided and the journey has to be planned much in advance. Without a proper map it becomes difficult to get to the destination. When we actually undertake the journey, if travellers in the compartment are sitting with gloomy faces, the journey becomes monotonous. On the other hand, if the environment is friendly or we make it friendly, the journey becomes pleasant.

Similarly life is a journey, a long one. The basics are the same. We should know the destination i.e. our goal. The stages of life are similar to stations during the journey. Like the journey, we should have proper planning for achieving the goals in life. We should know how to work with people and enjoy life. Finally, there has to be a proper strategy to execute the plan lest the journey remains only on paper. One's lifespan is not eternal. Therefore, there has to be a timetable for achieving goals.

The world is changing at a fast pace and society is also undergoing rapid changes. The present millennium is much different from the earlier ones. Life is not a smooth journey either. During the journey, there are speed breakers and bumps every now and then. We face many problems and challenges and there are different types of problems and challenges in terms of content and ferocity. The bigger the problem, the stake in the failure will also be big.

Life's problems do not wait indefinitely. If the problem is not tackled in time and it festers for a long time, there is every likelihood that it will appear later in a more complex form. One way of dealing with the problem is to deal right at the time when it occurs. However many a time we are caught unawares. The other way is to have a clear cut strategy in the form of a proactive approach so that the problem does not occur at all and even if it does it is not allowed to become so hard that it cannot be solved. The right strategy increases our efficiency exponentially as compared to a fire fighting approach.

For all practical purposes, a goal is an object of our effort; our destination. First we have to identify our purpose in life and then design a vision statement to enable us to achieve that purpose. The vision statement helps us to steer our course in life just like a rudder on a ship. The next in line is setting the goals. The goals are what we want to achieve. Ideally the goals have to be in alignment with our vision statement and the vision statement has to be in alignment with our purpose in life.

A goal gives a focus to use our potential and a road map to reach the destination. Setting a goal is the most effective way to achieve success. Importantly, being in the process of realization of a worthy goal gives us great happiness in life.

Some people may not realize the importance of setting goals because they might be living in an environment in which there is no such practice. The other reason could be they would not like to become responsible for the goals, because they remind us about our responsibility.

First of all we should try to know our purpose in life or what we wish to be. Then we have to find out how to realize it. We have to identify key areas of our life which have significant influence over us and indicate the direction in which we will have to move in those areas. The key areas of life are: Physical (health), Social / interpersonal (family, friends and inter personal relationship), Professional (working in organization) and Spiritual (connecting with real self / Almighty). Keeping the objective in view, we will have to prepare a vision statement just like the directive principles of the Indian Constitution.

From the guiding principles mentioned in our vision statement, the goals will flow, which means if goals are getting achieved, the guiding principles in the statement are being followed. It also means that we are perfectly in alignment with our purpose in life.

The vision encompasses broadly the following areas:

Physical (health) development
Social (family & friends) development
Professional (working in organization) development

Philanthropic nature
Spiritual (faith in real self / Almighty) development

Everybody has a view about the vision to fulfill the purpose of life. These would differ from person to person. I have attempted to give below my own personal vision.

- follow natural laws of health
- bring harmony and happiness in the family
- help friends in times of their need
- find my personal growth in the organization's growth
- work for uplifting lives of rural folk
- supplement the efforts of institutions I am associated with
- write book(s) on positive aspects of life
- enjoy living every moment of life as it comes
- listen to my inner self when the situation calls for it
- have unconditional faith in the Almighty.

Everybody should try to put down on paper his own vision statement. It should reflect personal choices rather than somebody else's.

Our goals have to be in line with our purpose of life and our vision statement. Otherwise we would be spending our valuable time and energy for something that may not be worthwhile to us. Also these goals should be found entirely by us and not designed by somebody else for us, as otherwise there will be no commitment from our heart to achieve the goals.

To this end we should prepare our wish list which means finding our wants. Some of these will be of a tangible nature and some will be intangible. Every goal should be measurable and a time frame for achieving it has to be fixed. Howsoever hard we may try there would be difficulty in measuring intangible goals. The only way out is to make them measurable to the extent that it is practically possible.

The goals should be realistic and achievable. If one is not in politics right now and one sets the goal to become President or Prime Minister of a country, it would be too unrealistic. Perhaps one may have to start with becoming a member of a political party or float one's own party. This will be his first goal. However, there could be some exceptions to this criterion.

To sum up, the goals will emerge from our fantasies, dreams, wants, desires, needs etc. These will have to be evaluated with reference to their usefulness, practicability, and more importantly subtlety. Finally they will have to be weighed with reference to our potential and then if required we may have to take a thoughtful chance.

Howsoever much we wish and make efforts to fulfill our want, it is not necessary that the same would be fulfilled. If we have faith in God, He will guide us to realize only that want which is good for us. We should therefore always seek His guidance when any desire or want wells up in our mind.

Visions and goals can be put down in the following manner.

Vision is to	Goal is to
follow natural laws of health	leave smoking and alcohol by 31st March ...(year)
bring harmony and happiness in the family	organize celebration of birth anniversary of oldest member of family with gusto on 25th April ... (year)
help friends in times of their need	offer a loan of Rs. 50,000/- to a friend on 30th May .... (year) for his daughter's marriage ceremony

find my personal growth in the organization's growth	get a promotion when I complete a project on 15th June .... (year)

In line with our finding of the purpose of life and vision statement, we can now put down the goals along with the realistic timeframe for achieving them in a typical table shown below. The reader is free to choose both format and the contents therein as he deems fit. The idea is that the purpose of life, vision statement and the goals are person specific and therefore they should reflect one's own perspective. .

Goals	*Physical (health) development*	*Social (family & friends) development*	*Professional development*	*Philanthropic nature*
# 1				
# 2				
# 3				
# 4				
# 5				

Goals can be different for different people. It depends upon one's own belief. These vary from happiness to personal well being i.e. health, prosperity, children's well being, human welfare, completion of particular project and so on. According priority to a goal is the individual's choice. However, looking to the recent trend, generally personal happiness, health and success in career are topping the agenda.

The important aspect of setting our goals is that we should find our aptitude and choose our profession accordingly. The chances of success in such a profession are bright. However not all may be fortunate in getting a profession of one's choice. In such a case we should make extra efforts to develop our interest in the profession we are in.

The next thing is we should have a vision of growth. People set different goals. Some set one particular goal and all of their energy is concentrated in achieving it. On the other hand some people work on a group of goals and spread their energy to achieve as many goals as possible. If the goal is achieved, it brings acclaim from society. But there is also risk of failure. Further there are umpteen cases wherein these persons get "burnt out" due to the extreme effort they have to make to achieve the single goal. Families can get neglected and family life disturbed.

Levels of aspirations can be classified into three, namely ideal, minimum (not below certain level) and realistic. Then there are dream aspirations. The line between dream and ideal aspirations is thin but it is there. Everybody sets his level of aspirations in his own way. Situations vary according to the fields one finds oneself in.

How to accomplish the goal

Visualization is one of the unique faculties possessed by the human being. Visualization helps us to get the image of what we wish to create. If our goal is to build a house, we will have its image in our mind. When the idea first strikes a person's mind, it is to the extent that he wishes to have a house. In previous houses he might have come across many shortcomings, which he would like to avoid. He gets an idea in mind as to how the house should look. However, all these ideas will be hazy. As he gains consciousness, the hazy ideas start getting proper sizes. He makes an outline and then he starts making a design. The design will follow his image. He checks up involuntarily the fact that the size and content of the house are commensurate with his financial capacity.

There are many people who do not make efforts to give practical shape to their hazy ideas. They remain hazy all the time. They try to fix the goal but they do not have any clarity about the goal.

Vision is imaginative insight. A visionary is the person who is aware of the big picture he wants to create and then works ceaselessly to create it. This big picture is part of the fulfillment of the purpose of life. All great men have been visionaries. They could visualize the event that is to come in the future. Their vision showed them the path and guided their journey of life. Their vision led them to reach great heights. Clear vision of the purpose of our life and our goals enable the events to happen.

Goals are means to accomplish our vision and thus fulfill the purpose of our life. Goals give us a focus for concentrating our effort. If we do not set the goals before us, our energy will be frittered away in abstract thinking and doing unimportant work. Setting a goal is a scientific process. It should neither be overambitious nor below our true potential. It should be somewhat above our potential so that we stretch ourselves to achieve higher and higher performance level. The visualization of the ultimate picture about what we want to happen helps us to formulate the goals. There should be enough clarity about the goal and then all our energy has to be focused on achieving the goal.

"People are always blaming their circumstances for what they are. I don't believe in circumstances. The people who get on in this world are the people who get up and look for the circumstances they want, and, if they can't find, make them."

George Bernard Shaw

TWELVE
The Key to Success

Success and failure

Success means accomplishment of aim or favorable outcome. Success can mean different things to different people.

The measurement of success depends upon a person and his perception. If success is being measured by self, sense of fulfillment when the aim is achieved will be the criterion. If some other person is measuring the success, he may view it from his own angle. In the latter case one's aim will not be the reference point. If the criterion in both the cases is similar, it is fine. If there is a variation and if one looks from the other's point of view about one's success or failure, there could be a real problem. In this case even if he has accomplished his aim, he may not derive a full sense of fulfillment, if he is led by another's opinion.

Every person will define success in his own way as he is the only person who determines what success means to him. As he moves forward, does not get stuck with the obstacles and derives a sense of fulfillment for his sincere efforts, it will mean success to him.

Success should bring harmonious results to us. If somebody is wealthy but his health is poor, he will not be able to enjoy his wealth. Similarly if one has health but one has not developed one's mental faculty, one will not be happy. Success should therefore encompass all the human faculties. Broadly speaking, success is that which enables us to derive personal satisfaction while pursuing it.

Some people tend to fear failure assuming that they will never succeed. Failure is a step in the direction of long-term success. Failure does not mean we have wasted our efforts. We learn a lot from failure and this experience is very helpful when we renew our efforts.

Failures, setbacks, disappointments should be considered as challenges to be responded with improved ability i.e. with "Response-ability". Most champions in sports or businesses faced rough weather due to several failures in the initial period of their career. The stories of their successes are replete with a common characteristic and that is they did not focus too much on their failures but utilized valuable experience out of the failures to readjust their strategies for attaining success.

Michael Johnson, the legendary figure in basketball, had to initially face failure in not getting a place in the school basketball team. But he didn't give up his efforts to get into the team again. If he had, the world would have been poorer by missing the delight his game provided.

Those who participated but could not succeed have learnt something new. A classic example of success and failure is the job search nowadays which poses quite a challenge to youth. Though there are several avenues for employment, it is not easy to get jobs on account of stiff competition. The aspirants, who seek employment and whose qualification, experience and aptitude generally meet the criteria as declared by the employer, participate in the process of selection. As only a few of the participants are expected to be selected, should others feel that their efforts have gone in vain? Not at all.

It is a process of selection in which not all eligible candidates can be accommodated by the employer. The persons who could not be selected should have a fair amount of satisfaction that they have sincerely tried for the selection and they have also learnt something new in the process.

Key elements of success

Nowadays the word success is one of the most widely used in the context of personality development. However we should be clear about the area in which we are trying to seek success. Generally the reference points for measuring success are goals that are set by us.

In essence our goals have to be in line with our purpose of life and our vision statement.

Goals are evolved from our wants. The wants which we are using quite often or wants based upon their utility and our affordability are our wants. The acid test of setting the goals is that they should be worth the effort we put in.

The goals should be realistic and achievable in the sense that they should be related to resources, efforts and time that we can provide or generate.

Opportunities are openings for new options offered by circumstances. If we are alert, keep our eyes and ears open, we all too often will come across some or the other opportunities for our progress.

We are normally skeptical about saying "yes" to opportunities which are hard in nature, because we are reluctant to work outside our comfort zone. But the greatest pay off is in the opportunities which are hard in nature. Those who want to succeed in life should be prepared to take on such opportunities. Further, opportunities may initially seem to cause or may actually cause disturbance to our set lifestyle but they can also offer us a new way of life which may be exhilarating.

Person A with a positive mental attitude will always like to work on the opportunity. He is prepared to take a reasonable risk and work harder to get success. On the other hand person B with a negative mental attitude will find many excuses for not getting anywhere near the opportunity. Person B will always like to identify himself with a general lot. Person A will not mind becoming odd man out if he is convinced about the viability of the opportunity.

The feeling of interest and enjoyment in one's work is the outcome of positive thinking. It has no direct relationship with the amount of money one gets as a remuneration for doing the work. We will find these people working with the same spirit under any circumstances, easy or hard.

There is a popular story on the subject being discussed. At one place three workers were engaged in breaking the stones. A passerby asked one of them, "What are you doing?" The worker said, "Are you not seeing I am breaking the stones?" He asked another worker the same question. That worker replied, "I am breaking the stones to earn money for my livelihood." He then repeated the question to third worker. That worker replied, "I am breaking the stones for building a church here." All three workers were engaged in the same work but the perception of each towards the work was different.

The expression of "can't do or" "impossible" belongs to a person who indulges in negative thinking and negative thinking stems from disbelief in one's real self. He may then form an opinion that he is not capable of doing things right. Such disbelief amounts to passing a decree against ourselves in the beginning itself. On the other hand, a person of positive thinking will persist in his efforts and he will always be ready to give his best in any situation.

The thoughts in our conscious mind are always influenced by our subconscious mind. If we succeed at doing something, we may remember it for sometime. However if we fail and we harbor defeatist thoughts for a long time, these are grooved deeply in our subconscious. These find expression whenever we come across some problem. Our entrenched belief that we are bound to fail tries to make things happen that way. On the other hand, if we saturate our subconscious with the thoughts that with our best efforts and the help of God we are going to succeed, there are ninety nine percent chances that we will succeed. There is an intimate relationship between thinking and the results that flow.

Any scheme we take in hand will face some problem or the other. The problems will vary according to the size of the schemes. If the scheme is bigger, there may be more problems. As a good planner we should be in a position to anticipate these problems.

There is a slight difference between will power and passion in the context in which we are using these words here. While both relate to strong desire, passion includes an element of emotion. The road to achieve great things is not easy. Had it been so easy, everybody would have climbed Mt. Everest. You will meet many challenges such as difficult terrain, inclement weather, snow storms etc., on the way to success. To get the results or the fruit out of them, we will have to pay the necessary price in terms of toil. We should have strong will power for achieving something good and worthwhile. If we have a will power emanating straight from the heart and we are steadfast in facing those challenges, we are sure to win. We should never give in, in spite of reverses.

Things don't come easily. We have to work for them. It is difficult to accomplish any worthwhile goal unless we are passionate about it and pursue it wholeheartedly. Undreamt of energy flows when we become interested in the work. The goal may be great or the objective pious but unless our interest to accomplish them is total, we are most likely to miss it. Interest makes things easy.

Concentration, confidence and courage are three qualities which should always be cultivated if one wishes to attain success in one's life. Likewise, capacity to take risks, commitment in working towards our goal, and infinite patience make for progress and hence success. Being responsible in whatever work we undertake, not blaming others, displaying steadfastness and motivation are surely likely to propel us towards success.

Broader meaning and purpose of success

While we should try to do things as best as possible, we should not be after perfection. Perfection in anything is mostly impractical. Some people are obsessed with the idea of perfection and when they are unable to achieve it they become restless. To attempt perfection is imposing unrealistic standards on ourselves. Strangely they not only expect perfection in whatever they do but they expect similar standards from others too. Imposition of such standards impossible to attain, makes these people remain always discontented.

Unfortunately the people who are obsessed with perfection are prone to make more mistakes. The expectation of perfection either from us or from others is many a time responsible for disharmony in families and social life. They remain always stressed and are unable to enjoy life. Quite often due to expectation of perfection from others, they make others' life also miserable. It is better to believe in the concept that we should do things as best as possible and leave them there. This will take pressure off from the mind and one would be able to enjoy work as well as life to the brim.

A smile on the face has the power to communicate with others which no other characteristic has. It communicates how well you feel when you see the other person, your interest in the other person. It is contagious as the other person is most likely to reciprocate by a smile. When a child smiles its effect spreads like the fragrance of a flower. The entire atmosphere becomes pleasant. There is no other way to impress somebody as giving a smile. A smile improves our facial expression. That is why while taking photographs, the photographer always says, "smile please." In business especially there is no other potent way as a smile for the sales person to please the customer. It costs nothing to the sales person and enriches the receiver.

Success is a continuing process and it has no finish line: When we achieve a goal we think that we have achieved success. However it will be a wrong proposition to think that there is nothing more to be achieved. The success that we have achieved pertains to one of the infinitesimal aspects, fields or areas of our life. When viewed from the point of success of a goal that is already achieved, we will sight another fascinating aspect, field or area, which we will choose for achievement. Accordingly we will set the goals and start our efforts all over again. Thus success is a never ending process.

When somebody gets success in one area of business, he may expand his business in the same area or he may enter into an entirely new area of business. Those who have accumulated a lot of money or even those who might not, may turn to philanthropic activity. After a certain age, one may like to focus on keeping good health and take it easy on other aspects of life. Having achieved many things in material world, some may turn to spiritual aspects. If we take a view from one peak of the mountain, soon we will see another peak and we will then set that peak as our destination. There is nothing like if we achieve a particular point of success, we will have no more to achieve. As soon as we achieve success in one area we will choose another area. It is thus impossible to define finality of success. The definition of success keeps on changing every time we achieve one.

In our pursuit to achieve success, although the final point of success gives us happiness, the journey on the way to that point too offers an opportunity for enjoyment. Rather if we skip the viewpoints during the journey to success, the journey itself will become unpleasant and there will be much less happiness left at the destination. It is just the same as in the case of our climbing to the top of the mountain. On the trail, there are several locations from which we get beautiful views of the scenery around. If we miss the scenery from those locations, we will be missing an important part of the whole journey. The happiness at the peak will then give us part happiness. For the total happiness we will have to enjoy the whole journey.

Thus, success is a process. It is a lifelong continuing process striving for different or better achievements. It is a never ending one. It has got to be like this as we cannot sit on our past laurels. Even otherwise, if we choose not to be part of the process, we will remain stagnant and we will encounter a different set of problems, which in all probability may be more severe than if we would have chosen focusing on some area of positive activity.

It is generally said that the whole world is moving with faith. Faith is an essence of our life. Depending upon the ethical approach in relationship, each of us derives strength from the others in whom we put faith. However, the greatest of all the sources of strength is God, Creator of our world. Once we repose faith in Him, nothing is to be feared. He is the greatest giver and healer. He has put soul, His spirit, in our body and guides us through intuition or inner voice. However we have to carefully listen to that intuition or the inner voice. No matter how great are the difficulties, with our sincere efforts to solve those difficulties and keeping faith in Him, we are bound to succeed in life. This success may or may not be purely in material form, but it will certainly be All-Round Success and that is what should rightly be our aim.

To conclude, success means accomplishment of aim or favorable outcome. It can mean different things to different people as their aims or the measure of outcome could be different. Success is a never ending process. We tend to feel that once we get a good job, the success in life is achieved. But it does not happen that way. Once we are successful in getting a job we wanted, another area is waiting for us and that is how to become a successful leader. Success and failure are part of our life. We should utilize the experience of failure for avoiding similar failure in future. Although we should give enough thought before we act, such an exercise should not lead to procrastination. Proactive approach helps us to avoid many problems that crop up later. Positive mental attitude, patience, perseverance and discipline in our life are prerequisites for success in our life.

"My religion consists of a humble admiration of the illimitable superior spirit who reveals himself in the slight details we are able to perceive with our frail and feeble minds."

Albert Einstein

THIRTEEN
Self-Realisation: The Goal

Purpose of Life

How do we visualize our role on this planet or real purpose of life? When our mind is peaceful and if we go deep within, we will have an idea of it. Even without ourselves being aware, our thinking and actions to a varying degree are influenced by it.

The purpose of life may be different for different people. In the spiritual field, realization of self is generally said to be the purpose of life. Other purposes of life could be: being a good (well behaved) human being; serving the needy in the society; learning and getting enlightened throughout life; leading happy and contented life. The list can become longer and longer as everybody recognizes the purpose as per his own highest calling. When we talk about purpose, it is understood that it will be oriented in a constructive way. Nobody should be finding killing somebody as his purpose of life even if that somebody may be his enemy.

Each human being is born with a few unique qualities among others. We should recognize these unique qualities as the same help us to fulfill our purpose in life.

Sometimes our thinking and actions might have been in alignment with the purpose of life and sometimes not. Once we become aware of our purpose of life, all our thinking and actions can be directed so as to be generally in alignment with that purpose. The purpose will then be like a north pole to the compass. It will constantly remind us about the direction we are moving in and the direction which was intended for our journey of life!.

If we can afford to choose a career which is in alignment with our purpose, it is the best thing to happen. However if for practical reasons this is not possible, we should strive to align all our activities to the purpose as soon as possible. We can also look beyond our profession about fulfilling the purpose.

Generally it is preferable if we keep the purpose of life known to us alone and do not announce it to others. If anybody happens to know about it, he may infer that our thinking and actions seem to be dictated by that specific purpose and therefore our actions are not in tune with their thinking. The purpose is then perceived as leading to conflict of interests. Notwithstanding this aspect, many thinkers let it be known to others because they are not perturbed by others' opinions.

Real Self/higher power

Of all things in the world, understanding the self is the most important aspect of personal development. Understanding the self would involve knowing one's personal traits, potentialities, weaknesses and strengths. Interestingly it is easier for a person to find in others, their qualities especially their shortcomings. It is therefore quite useful to hear criticism of oneself from others if one wants to improve. However rather than depending on others, the best way of understanding the real self is by contemplation at the end of the day as to how one had performed during the day. Here contemplation means self-analysis in an objective manner. To do self-analysis in objective manner, one requires understanding of what is positive or negative thinking and what is right or wrong action in different circumstances. In this respect, God has been favourable to a human being as he has been endowed with a distinct power of discrimination to know what is right and what is wrong. However this power of discrimination has to be developed by experience and practice of doing things in the right manner.

Subtle values

There is a big difference between just living and leading a meaningful life. What is meaningful life? The answer to this question is again related to what is the purpose of life and why we were born. Most of us want to lead the life as it happens because in that case no special effort is required. However if we wish to lead a purposeful living, we will have to follow certain principles. Since one has to make certain sacrifices while following these principles, not many people are prepared to follow the path of principles. For example, those living in Gandhiji's ashram had to lead a life of utmost austerity and discipline.

There are many people who are quite knowledgeable. They advise people to follow certain ethics in life. But they themselves do not follow the same thing in their life. We should strive to live up to our principles. Only then will there be congruency between our thinking and actions. People will then trust what we say. However, there is no doubt that in this complex world, it is not easy to live up to our principles. But then it is worthwhile to strive for them.

There is a story about Gandhiji. A woman approached Gandhiji along with her son. She told Gandhiji that her son was strongly addicted to eating sugar and sought Gandhiji's help to wean him away from eating too much of sugar. Gandhiji told her to come after a month. When she came after a month, he told her to come after another one month. Like this six months passed. At the end of six months, Gandhiji quietly told her son to avoid eating sugar. Surprisingly her son stopped eating sugar. His mother wondered why Gandhiji took six months just to say a sentence to her son. Gandhiji told her that he was himself trying to stop eating sugar and he found that it was difficult for him to stop eating sugar. It took him full six months to stop eating sugar. Only after attaining self control he thought he could advise her son to give up eating sugar. Till then he thought he had no moral authority to advise another person about something which he himself was not able to follow.

According to Gandhiji, the things that will destroy us are:

"Wealth without work
Pleasure without conscience
Knowledge without character
Commerce without morality
Science without humanity

Worship without sacrifice
Politics without principle"

According to Gandhiji, ends cannot justify means i.e. means to achieve the ends are as important (i.e. should be pure) as the ends to be achieved.

Based on our beliefs we hold certain values as most dear to us. As long as our beliefs are rational, values chosen by us are bound to be positive and they will aid our development. However these values, instead of keeping them in abstract terms, should form part of our culture so that these are practiced in day to day life situations.

There are natural laws which govern the life of human beings. If we break these laws we do it at our own peril. These laws are based upon reality and truth and the same are true for all time. It is necessary to implement these laws in real life situations for the happiness and prosperity of the family or the society.

Certain observances flow from the natural laws. These are stated by Patanjali, a Hindu sage as:

Yama- 1. Satya (Truth); 2. Ahimsa (Non-injury); 3. Bramhacharya (Celibacy); 4. Asteya (Non-stealing); 5. Aparigraha (Non-possession) or Non-covetousness

& Niyama- 1. Purity of mind & body; 2. Contentment in all circumstances; 3. Self discipline; 4. Contemplation (self-study); 5. Devotion to Creator/God.

Some people who live in a confined area start thinking themselves great just as kings and queens of smaller areas in the past used to think of themselves. These highly egoistic people create their imaginary world. They think they know everything and are wisest in the world. They feel they are legends. The egoistic people don't mind giving unsolicited advice to anybody, anywhere, anytime. They are attention seeking. They have a craze for crowds to be around them. They always try to dominate discussions whether they know the subject under discussion or not. They are always on the lookout for an audience. Except for flatterers, people try to avoid such egoistic persons.

We do many things to satisfy our ego irrespective of the fact that we may be hurting others in the process. We should therefore always keep our ego under control. However it is always good to carry a feeling of self worth on the basis of what we have achieved and what we are set to achieve. There is a world of difference between 'being egotist or having vanity' and 'having a feeling of self-worth'. While the former has a negative connotation, the latter is positive. To have a feeling of self worth is the key to human personality and success. If we expand our self worth, we expand our ability to succeed in larger areas.

Self worth allows us to learn from our weaknesses and get over them instead of getting overwhelmed by them. Self worth keeps us protected from self doubt that often tries to sneak in our mind.

Unless we believe in our real self, how can we expect others to believe in us? Unless we have confidence in ourselves, how can others have confidence in us? Even if the whole world does not believe you, but if you believe in your real self, one day people will believe in you. The first step to success in life is to have belief in our real self. Without this one essential element, all other abilities will not be effective.

The tender age is like a clean slate. There is nothing written on it. Children form their ideas as parents or teachers teach them. Besides, what they learn from friends has a profound effect on them. Having no first hand experience of the world, there is abundant curiosity in the minds of children. This abundant curiosity with no power of value judgment can lead them to unintended habits.

It is most beneficial if one develops good qualities and make them part of one's nature at an early age. In this context, it will be very helpful if ethical training is made available to younger generation at an early age.

The best way of self renewal is through connecting our self to our source of power i.e. our soul or real self. Self renewal can be achieved either through self effort by experience, through institutional retraining or through our mentors provided our mentors have themselves reached a good level of understanding.

Self-awareness is different from self-realization. Self-awareness is one of the important steps to self-realization. While self-realization is whole, self-awareness is part of that whole. We mean self-awareness here as awareness in the context of knowing what is good or bad for us.

Only human beings are endowed with the characteristic of self-awareness. Animals have awareness to the extent of needs for their survival-ability. They do have consciousness but they act according to instinct. In some circumstances human beings too act as animals when they lack in developing and utilizing this quality.

Personality, among other characteristics, is a combination of two important characteristics namely attitude and experience. Both are essential for development of one's personal growth. Although between the two, attitude is more important, attitude without experience does not take us too far in this competitive as well as complex world. On the other hand if one has experience but does not have a positive attitude, one will surely be a failure sooner or later.

Willingness to adapt to the environment in which we are placed should become part of our attitude so that if we find that our actions are not in tune with the calling of any situation, we should be ready to change ourselves to be in tune with new situations.

Honesty means being sincere, not lying, and earning by fair means. With growing competition, as a shortcut method to achieve, there is a tendency to adopt a manipulative approach, which may succeed in the short run. But in the long run such an approach will expose the person and he will lose his credibility and reputation. Many people use dishonesty as a shortcut to success. They lie even for small things. Afterwards lying becomes a habit. Self serving attitude makes them blind to see the truth. In course of time when other people come to know about their dishonesty, they despise these dishonest people.

Honesty is a quality to be nurtured. Honesty is no doubt not an easy path because many a time to keep the trust, which is a part of honesty, one has to suffer. When we give a word to somebody and then after sometime the circumstances change, to keep our word we might run into loss. But honesty pays in the long run because people would like to do business with the people who are honest. "Honesty is the best policy."

Integrity is wholeness which is more than honesty. Integrity should become part of our nature to become successful in life. It is impossible to succeed in the organization without having integrity towards the work we are engaged in and the people with whom we are working. The person of integrity may lack specialized knowledge. But organizations like to retain such people as long as possible and they place them in respectable positions.

Integrity and values are born out of conviction. Values could also be based on family and social ethos. Conviction is a product of our belief and personal experience. Thus integrity, values, conviction and belief are closely interrelated. They get reinforced or circumscribed by our personal experiences and compulsions when we conduct ourselves in life. However, unless these qualities represent expression of our real self, they can be sooner or later overpowered by irrationality.

Integrity means honesty, wholeness soundness. Thus integrity encompasses honesty. It is impossible to achieve anything worthwhile in life without cultivating integrity. Integrity can be towards achieving a goal/objective, personal life or even more importantly integrity towards oneself. Trust is a product of honesty and integrity. The person who has honesty and integrity is always trustful. Trust is a foundation of relationship or business. Honesty, integrity and trust build our character. Character is an essence of our life.

Faith: religious belief; creed; loyalty, trustworthiness

Just as we put faith in our parents, we have to have faith in religion. It is assumed here and rightly so that a religion is a way of life, it is a belief in a concept of tolerance and respecting the right of other people to choose the religion they wish to follow.

Many things get resolved and become easier if we relate ourselves with God. Some people may not believe in God but they may believe in some Superpower. When we talk about faith in God or Superpower, we mean that faith which impels us to work for the highest good of all concerned and not as self seeking exercise or idle thinking. Faith is not a reflection of weakness but a reflection of true strength. The test of faith is when we find in it solace in crises.

However when we refer faith with reference to Guru (spiritual teacher) we should first be sure that the Guru we have chosen can help us in making our knowing God easier.

It is not easy to find such Gurus. Those are geniuses and as such rare who can guide us in the spiritual field.

Let's also consider about the people who do not have faith in religion, God or Superpower. Many of them hold the opinion that as long as they do not do any harm to anybody and do right actions, there is no special need to think about belonging to a formal religion or believing in God. They feel by this way they would be spared of the rigidity which a faith in religion will bring in. I personally feel there is nothing wrong in this approach. But in practice, it would require a Herculean effort to maintain oneself on the right side. It becomes a lot more easier to keep us on the right side if we have faith in God and religion. Here faith does not mean blind faith.

Faith is believing that good things are going to happen. Faith represents hope and optimism. Faith in the broader sense is faith in the Almighty, faith in self or faith in all subtle things. Faith is the opposite of fear. Fear represents anxiety and worry. While faith is the real nature of human beings, fear robs man of his real nature. While faith in its process generates enthusiasm, fear diminishes strength. Fear makes a human being to take a defensive posture. While faith is invigorating, fear paralyzes. If we shed fear, we can work with ease. The very survival of the human race is based upon faith.

It is very difficult to concentrate on the work in hand if some serious conflicts are raging in our mind. These conflicts inhibit our ability of decision making. Therefore, these conflicts have to be resolved first and thoughts have to be harmonized. These conflicts could arise from the values which are dear to us or their interpretation. There are occasions when we are called upon to do something which is not congruent with the values we hold and hence conflicts arise. In such situations there is no better way than seeking guidance from our inner voice.

We should create a secret chamber of silence within our real self where we should not allow our moods, worries or inharmony to enter. In this chamber we can communicate with our inner self, Guru and God. We do enter this chamber every time when we are in meditation. Whenever we are disturbed by any unpleasant happening in the outside world, we should retire in this chamber. When we come out of the chamber, we are no more a disturbed person. We can then take things in our stride.

On happiness

Happiness is truly a very personal experience. There is no denying the fact that the socio-economic aspect does have influence on our happiness. However it is also certain that happiness does not depend so much upon external circumstances as it depends upon our internal state of mind. Happiness presupposes solution of day to day problems in a normal way. If we have positive state of mind, we find it a lot easier to find solutions to those problems. Thus, state of our mind or mental attitude largely determines our happiness.

Some people prefer to spend their whole life in doing things in a disinterested way. However there are also people who have some mission in their life and they work for that till the end. Their life becomes an inspiration for the seekers. They are always admired by the generations to come. What is the force driving them to achieve such greatness? If we have to sum up their common characteristics in two short words, these are Creative Wisdom; Creativity is the first and the foremost characteristic of a child which enables him to become a man, which unfortunately we lose gradually and steadily on the way as we age. The second one is wisdom which means knowledge, experience, prudence, and the resolve to apply them in our real life situations. The combination of these two characteristics has a potential to enable any human being to achieve great things in life.

If we keep all our achievements, successes, riches confined to ourselves, its tantamount hording. Unfortunately many of us are stuck with this instinct. God has given all things with a certain purpose. We are just trustees in the words of Gandhiji. As human beings, we are supposed to share them with the needy fellow beings who are not as fortunate like us. Riches are not the only things, which are to be shared. Even giving some of our knowledge, time, attention, compassion to help somebody in need is also the way to sharing. The opportunities for sharing may come in natural course without seeking them formally. We have only to be conscious to pick them up as they come.

Great souls like Mother Teresa, Gandhiji and several others adopted altruism as a way of life. It gave them immeasurable inner satisfaction. It is said that whatever we give will come back to us manifold. It may not come to us immediately. It can also be in invisible form like a healthy life. Brightening other's path may bring more brightness to our path.

Compassion or sympathy should be based upon a feeling of equality about the person whom we are trying to help. It should not be construed as a favor to him to satisfy our ego, but as a moral duty towards another human being.

The person who has some resources is supposed to share with others who may lack the same and vice a versa. This phenomenon is give and take. However human relations call for more considerate approach than keeping a count of how much is to be given and how much is to be taken. The person who has enough resources can afford to give to the needy without expecting a return. Here generosity implies that the person with resource can take a still bigger view and offer help without expecting a matching return.

Can we imagine the count of what and how much assistance is to be given by each in the intimate relationships like between parents and child, between spouses and between friends? Certainly not! Such relationship either transcends or should transcend the count. We can further expand our base and similarly include others. However this does not mean it should be one sided affair. This would be straight unreasonable. If it is felt that there is unfairness in giving and receiving, the same should be resolved to the satisfaction of both the parties involved.

Life consists of trials, tribulations, failures, opportunities, wonders, successes and so on. If we hold a positive attitude towards life, our journey of life becomes much easier. Trials, tribulations and failures will then be transformed into opportunities, wonders and successes. If we take this process further and feel gratitude for everything in life, life will become a joy for us. Obviously our greatest gratitude is towards the Creator.

Leaving a legacy behind

Man is creative by nature. Some people think they should create only such things that last during their lifetime. They feel they would in any case not be there to see or enjoy the things after death, then why should they create? However some people take a view that our forefathers, who fought for their as well as their families' survival in most difficult times, left behind so many things that their offspring now find life easier. Ancestral people are remembered for good things that they have left behind for the next generation.

Leaving a legacy behind means what is it that we are leaving behind after our death for which we would be remembered. Obviously one would always like to be remembered for the good things.

Unique qualities are those which set a person apart from others. There are many activities one does routinely. But there are some activities which arouse more interest, give more personal happiness in doing those activities. One finds these activities more interesting and one is happier to do these because one finds expression of one's unique qualities in these activities. Thus one can trace unique qualities from the activities which interest him and give more personal happiness to him. These activities may or may not be the ones which are part of his profession. In fact one is very fortunate if he is in the profession which comprises predominantly these activities.

Learning, creating and growing:

The process of leaving a legacy behind has to be preceded by sustained effort to develop our unique qualities and in this respect there can be no better teacher in the world than learning from the child. Learning, creating and growing are the three basic characteristics of a child. We need to nurture these qualities throughout our life.

A child is fond of learning new things. Their observation is very keen. Once they observe us pressing the switch for the tube-light, they know that for making the tube-light, glow first a switch located at a particular place has to be pressed. We learn a lot if we pay attention to what is happening around us. This faculty should not be dispensed with even in old age because its utility is increasing in the present age of the internet. Many technological advancements are taking place, which have tremendous influence on our day to day lives.

The child wants to explore and create new things. We have to nurture this urge. The present stage of development is a result of evolution for millions of years and evolution is a continuous process. It will go on creating new things. In the scheme of things we will have no place if we keep ourselves stagnant.

Development has to be overall development. The urge for growing should not be diminishing with increasing age. The process of learning, creating and growing is a continuing process and age has no bearing on this process.

Life is a journey. There is no final destination for this journey. It's not some point and no further. Our journey stops only when our final call comes. Life is not full of roses all the time. It comprises both successes and failures. There is no finish line to fulfilling life. We can't say we have achieved whatever was to be achieved and there is nothing more to be achieved, and now we want to take rest till the final call comes. Many people particularly who are retired from employment tend to feel that way. They feel they have gone through a tough time and now they would like to take rest.

However life means activity. It may be physical or mental or both. If there is no activity, disuse phenomenon takes over. The house which remains unused for a long period deteriorates faster and lastly crumbles. The water which remains stagnant for a long time stinks and becomes a source of disease. Our body if not kept in use loses its vitality and over a period of time will start decomposing. Similarly if we don't use our mental faculty properly, we will lose basic functions like cognition or memory. Our living will be similar to vegetation. Therefore activity is an essence of life. A choice of right activity as a part of goal achievement will mean we are moving in a right direction and a choice of negative activity will mean we are moving in a wrong direction. It depends entirely on us which way we choose.

Biologically our body cells undergo degeneration with aging. The process of degeneration of cells can be slowed down by adopting a healthy lifestyle in the form of keeping involved in right activity, exercise, proper diet, healthy environment and rest. Although awareness about maintenance of good health and medical breakthroughs in many fields have contributed to increasing average lifespan, thus far no way has been found either to reverse the process of degeneration or even to stay put further degeneration of cells. If a way is found, the man will have no death.

There is however a silver lining to the process. Contrary to the earlier belief, the latest research fortunately indicates that, in spite of age, the brain cells also regenerate as other cells of the body. Therefore if we take care of our mental and physical faculties, (more so) mental faculty will be giving us company for a pretty long time. There are many people who though weak in physical body have mental faculties functioning well past the age of 70 years. The question naturally arises whether normal pace of degeneration in physical body and slow pace of degeneration of mental faculty will be helpful for us or not. Although our capacity to handle physical work will diminish, we may still be able to function with our less affected mental faculties.

We are born on this earth with a certain purpose. The outcome of fulfilling that purpose is supposed to make our world a better place to live in. Everybody is endowed with certain unique qualities which set him apart from others. By developing these qualities, a person is in a position to contribute to the welfare of the society including his own and thus fulfill the purpose of his life.

Our life is full of complexities. Our journey through life consists of pleasant as well as unpleasant experiences. During our journey, we may encounter tough problems as well as failures. The appropriate approach to solve those problems and failures has been given in this book. It is my firm belief that there is no problem or failure on this earth, which cannot be solved with our sincere and sustained efforts coupled with faith in a Higher Power i.e. God.

APPENDIX

The effectiveness of affirmations for betterment of a man is based on the simple principle that man becomes what he constantly thinks. By repetition the affirmations make deeper grooves in the brain. The affirmations constitute positive ideas. Therefore, affirmations help us to concentrate on positive thinking. We should prepare affirmations which are specific as well as convincing to us. I give below the affirmations which have been prepared by me for myself. I find reciting these affirmations everyday in the morning helps me to maintain positive thinking throughout the day.

- I am submerged in eternal light. It permeates every particle of my being. I am in that light. The Divine Spirit fills me within and without. Our lives are the reflection of that Spirit. No wave can exist without the ocean behind it; so we must realize the great ocean of life throbbing behind our lives.
- I am eternal youth; I am health; I am strength; I am joy; I am successful, I am peace, I am immortal

- Within me is the infinite Creative Power. I shall not leave this world without some accomplishments. I am a God-man, a rational man. I am the power of Spirit, the dynamic Source of my soul. I shall create revelations in the world of action, in the world of thought, in the world of wisdom. I and my Father are One. I can create anything I desire, even as my creative Father.
- God has given me the power of thinking and action. However my responsibility for entertaining particular thoughts and actions is absolute. Therefore instead of relating the effects on fate or destiny, I will use my discrimination carefully and entertain only such thoughts and take such actions which are subtle in nature and reflect my real self. However I have faith in God that He would continue to guide me throughout my life.
- I will, to the best of my ability, not only utilize but also work for expansion of the unique gifts i.e. health, prosperity etc. bestowed on me by Him and thus will redeem the trust placed by Him in me.
- O Father, I want prosperity, health and wisdom without measure, not from earthly sources but from Thine all-possessing, all powerful, all bountiful hands.
- I will be neither lazy nor feverishly active. In every challenge of life I shall do my best without worrying about the future, since worrying only compounds the problem
- While senses may lure, indulgence in them does not give durable happiness. On the other hand they pull us down deeper and deeper into the gorge. Perceive what subtle and fleeting pleasure and health and disease, are below the surface rather than going by

the pull of the senses. Go still deeper and you will find Atman in whom there is no difference between man and woman.

- While I will continue to strive for my growth, I will have full measure of contentment in whatever circumstances I am placed. Neither does contentment inhibit growth nor is non-contentment a necessary condition to spur personal growth.
- I form new habits of thinking by seeing good everywhere, and by beholding all things as the perfect idea of God made manifest.
- Others deserve same freedom of perception as I expect for myself.
- Whenever a feeling of anger or disliking overtakes me, instead of reacting instantaneously, I will give a pause to frame my most proper response to the situation.
- I will carry no feeling of ill will or hatred toward anybody as all of us are children of God; However I will keep away from their ideas and actions which according to my inner voice will come in the way of my progress as a pilgrim.
- I have a special relationship with my wife who had borne my idiosyncrasies and stood with me in most difficult times.
- It is unfortunate that some unpleasant happening has taken place, but there is no guarantee that this must not happen. Hence accept it, learn from it and move ahead.
- I will be careful about accident and fall as they may change the course of my life.
- As I radiate love and goodwill to others especially the underserved, I will open the channel for God's love to come to me.

(Footnote: Some of the affirmations here have been taken from the book, *Where There Is Light,* a compendium of selections from the teachings of Sri Sri Paramahansa Yogananda, founder of Yogoda Satsanga Society of India)

BIBLIOGRAPHY

Armstrong, Thomas: *The Human Odyssey: Navigating the Twelve Stages of Life;* Sterling Publishing Co. Inc. New York, USA; 2007

Attwood, Janet Bray & Chris Attwood: *The Passion Test: The Effortless Path to Discovering Your Destiny;* Hudson Street Press; Penguin Group, New York, USA; 2007

Beazley, Hamilton: *No Regrets: A Ten - Step Program for Living in the Present and Leaving the Past Behind;* John Wiley & Sons, New Jersey, USA; 2004

Bhalla, Shahu, *Quotes of Gandhi;* UBS Publishers' Distributors Ltd, New Delhi, India; 1995

Brim, Gilbert: *Ambition: How We Manage Success and Failure Throughout Our Lives;* Basic Books, a Division of Harper Collins, USA; 1992

Canfield, Jack: *The Success Principles;* Harper Collins Publishers, New York, USA; 2007

Carlson, Richard: *Easier Than You Think: because Life Does Not Have to be so Hard, the Small Changes that Add Up to World of Difference;* Harper Collins Publishers. New York, USA; 2005

Carnegie, Dale: *Dale Carnegie's Lifetime Plan for Success- How to Win Friends & Influence People;* Galahad Books, New York, USA; 1998

Carnegie, Dale: *How to Stop Worrying & Start Living;* Galahad Books, New York, USA; 1998

Carter - Scott, Cherie *If Success Is a Game, These Are the Rules: Ten Rules for a Fulfilling Life;* Broadway Books, New York; 2000

Cloud, Henry: *9 Things You Simply Must Do: to Succeed in Love and Life;* Integrity Publishers, Brentwood, TN, USA; 2004

Colbert, Don: *Stress Less;* SILOAM; Lake Mary, Florida, USA; 2005

Colbert, Don: *The Seven Pillars of Health: The Natural Way to Better Health for Life;* SILOAM; Lake Mary, Florida, USA; 2006

Covey, Stephen R.: *The 7 Habits of Highly Effective People;* Free Press, a Division of Simon & Schuster, New York, USA; 1989, 2004

Covey, Stephen R.: *The 8th Habit: From Effectiveness to Greatness;* Free Press, a Division of Simon & Schuster, USA,New York; 2005

Dean, Ornish: *Program for Reversing Heart Disease;* IVY Books: New York, USA; 1996

Dewan, A. P: *Back to Nature for Healthy Living;* A. C. Specialist Publishers, New Delhi, India; 1988

Dyer, Wayne W.: *Change Your Thoughts- Change Your Life: Living the Wisdom of the Tao;* Hay House, Carlsbad, California, USA; 2007

Dyer, Wayne W.: *The Power of Intention;* Hay House, California, USA; 2004

Dyer, Wayne W.: *Wisdom of the Ages;* Harper Collins Publishers, New York, USA; 1998

Ellis, Albert & Arthur Lange: *How to Keep People from Pushing Your Buttons;* Carol Publishing Group; New York, USA; 1994

Ellis, Albert & Emmett Velten: *Optimal Aging: Get Over Getting Older;* Open Court Publishing Company, a Division of Carus Publishing Co. Peru, Illinois; 1998

Enright, Robert D.: *Forgiveness Is a Choice: A Step-by-Step Process for Resolving Anger and Restoring Hope;* APA Life Tools, American Psychological Association, Washington, DC, USA; 2001

Erikson, Erik H: (Homburger). *Identity and the Life Cycle;* W.W.Norton & Company, New York. London; c. 1959; c 1980

Erikson Erik H. *Identity: Youth and Crisis;* W.W.Norton & Company, Toronto, Canada; 1968

Freud, Sigmund (translated by A.A. Brill): *The Interpretation of Dreams;* Random House, New York, USA; 1994 (Modern Library Edition).

Heller, Rachael & Richard Heller: *Healthy Selfishness: Getting the Life You Deserve Without the Guilt;* Meredith Books; Des Moines, Iowa; USA; 2006

Hingorani, Anand T & Ganga A. Hingorani, *The Encyclopaedia of Gandhian Thoughts;* AICC, New Delhi; 1985

Jung, C.G. (translated by H.G.Baynes) *Psychological Types;* New York, Pantheon, USA; 1976

Jung, C.G. *The Undiscovered Self: with Symbols and the Interpretation of Dreams* Translated and Revised by R.F.C. Hull; Princeton University Press, New Jersey, USA; Erikson. 1990

Jussawala, J M: *The Natural Way of Healing;* Vikas Publishing House, New Delhi, India; 1974

Kirschenbaum, Howard & Valerie Land Henderson (eds) *Carl Rogers Dialogues;* Houghton Mifflin Company, Boston, USA

Kirshenbaum, Mira: *Everything Happens for a Reason: Finding the True Meaning of the Events in Our Lives;* Harmony Books, New York, USA; 2004

Leider, Richard J.: *The Power of Purpose: Creating Meaning in Your Life and Work;* Berrett- Koehler Publishers, San Francisco, USA; 1997

Madson, Patricia Ryan: *Improv Wisdom- Don't Prepare, Just Show Up;* Bell Tower, New York, USA; 2005

Manz, Charles C. *The Power of Failure: 27 Ways to Turn Life's Setbacks into Success;* Berrett- Koehler Publishers, San Francisco, USA; 2001

Maxwell, John C.: *Today Matters: 12 Daily Practices to Guarantee Tomorrow's Success;* Warner Faith, New York, USA; 2004

Maxwell, Maltz: *Psycho- Cybernetics: New Technique for Using Your Subconscious Power;* Melvin Powers, Wilshire Book Company, California, USA; 1960

McGraw, Phillip C.: *Life Strategies: Doing What Works, Doing What Matters;* Hyperion, New York, USA; 1999

McGraw, Phillip C.: *Real Life: Preparing for 7 Most Challenging Days of Your Life;* Free Press, a Division of Simon & Schuster, New York, USA; 2008

McKinney, Frank, *Make It Big: 49 Secrets for Building a Life of Extreme Success;* John Wiley & Sons, New York, USA; 2002

Pausch, Randy & Jeffrey Zaslow, *The Last Lecture;* Hyperion, New York, USA; 2008

Peale, Norman Vincent: *The Power of Positive Thinking;* Simon & Schuster, New York, USA; 1994

Pelzer, Dave: *Help Yourself :* Celebrating the Rewards of Resilience and Gratitude; A Dutton Book; Penguin Group, New York, USA; 2000

Rich, Harvey L. & Teresa Barker, *In the Moment;* Harper Collins Publishers, New York; USA; 2002

Roger, John & Peter McWilliams: *You Can't Afford the Luxury of a Negative Thought;* Prelude Press, Los Angeles, USA; 1990

Rogers, Carl R. *A Way of Being;* Houghton Mifflin Company, New York, USA: 1995

Schuller, Robert, Harold: *Success is Never Ending, Failure is Never Final;* Thomas Nelson Publishers, Nashville, USA; 1988

Scott Peck, M.: *The Road Less Travelled: A New Psychology of Love, Traditional Values and Spiritual Growth;* A Touchstone Book; Simon & Schuster, New York, USA; c. 1978, c 1985

Seligman, Martin E. P.: *What You Can Change & What You Can't:* The Complete Guide to Successful Self Improvement; Alfred A. Knopf, New York, USA; 1994

Sills, Judith: *Excess Baggage: Getting Out of Your Own Way;* Viking, Penguin Group, London, England; 1993

Storr, Anthony: *The Essential Jung; Selected Writings;* Princeton University Press, New Jersey, USA; 1983

Tichy, Noel M & Stratford Sherman: *Control Your Destiny or Someone Else Will;* Harper Business, a Division of Harper Collins, New York, USA; 1994

Tracy, Brian: *Goals: How to Get Everything You Want- Faster Than You Ever Thought Possible;* Berrett-Koehler Publishers, San Francisco, USA; 2002

Yogananda, Sri Sri Paramahansa: *Selections from the Teachings of Where There Is Light: Insight and Inspiration for Meeting Life's Challenges;* Yogoda Satsanga Society of India, Kolkata, India; 2002